A Sort of Columbus

The American Voyages of Saul Bellow's Fiction

Jeanne Braham

A Sort of Columbus

The American Voyages of

Saul Bellow's Fiction

The University of Georgia Press
Athens

Designed by Sandra Strother Hudson
Set in Linotron 202 Garamond with Galliard display
Printed in the United States of America

The paper in this book meets the guidelines
for permanence and durability of the Committee
on Production Guidelines for Book Longevity
of the Council on Library Resources.

Library of Congress Cataloging in Publication Data

Braham, Jeanne, 1940–
A sort of Columbus.

Bibliography: p.
Includes index.
1. Bellow, Saul—Criticism and interpretation.
I. Title.
PS3503.E4488Z58 1984   813'.52   83-10539
ISBN 0-8203-0690-8

"Why, I am a sort of Columbus
of those near-at-hand and believe
you can come to them in this immediate
terra incognita that spreads out in every
gaze. I may well be a flop at this line
of endeavor. Columbus too thought he was
a flop, probably, when they sent him back
in chains. Which didn't prove that there was
no America."

The Adventures of Augie March

Contents

Acknowledgments

Special thanks are due to Sue Braham Mullen, who early set a model of literary analysis worth reaching for; to Kristin Woolever, who read each version of this manuscript with steady insight; to Sonya Jones, who edited the book, taking down the partitions in my argument and making it whole; to Paul Zimmer, who supported the publication of the book in all the ways that matter.

My greatest debt is to the students of the Saul Bellow Seminars, 1972–1982, at Allegheny College. Their love of text and their provocative, often heated discussions offered the very best passport into Bellow's work. This is their book.

Introduction

Saul Bellow may well be American literature's most resourceful writer at present. He has come to his prominence slowly through a careful building up of a body of work, an *oeuvre* displaying greater insight, range, and power with each new novel.

In his work it is possible to trace a clear line of ideological and narrative development. He has advanced from the skeletal *Dangling Man* (1944) and the claustrophobic *The Victim* (1947), books that describe the nature of man's fixity in modern experience, to the expansive breakthrough of *The Adventures of Augie March* (1953), the intensity of *Seize the Day* (1956), and the exuberance of *Henderson the Rain King* (1959), books that explore the nature of man's freedom. The rich complexity of *Herzog* (1964), the organicism of *Mr. Sammler's Planet* (1970), the ambition of *Humboldt's Gift* (1975) and *The Dean's December* (1982) suggest a wholeness of vision: man must charge himself with understanding the nature of the experience that he rejects as well as of that which he affirms in order to live in the full recognition of his life's worth.

Bellow's narratives tell the tale of modern man in America, his terror in the face of dissolving reason, his persistent will to alter his destiny, his desire to reaffirm the values of community in an age where loyalties are fickle and allegiances to life are undertaken in the face of flimsy, often conflicting evidence. Bellow persistently refuses to devalue the self even in the midst of the "pressure of a vast public life." He writes, "One would have to be optimistic to the point of imbecility to raise the standard of pure affirmation and cry 'yea, yea' shrilly against the deep background of 'nays.'"[1] But as he says in his Library of Congress address, "One would like to ask {Sartre, Ionesco, Beckett, Burroughs, Ginsberg] 'After nakedness, what?' 'After absurdity, what?'"[2] So Bellow affirms; he attacks the "Wastelander,"[3] the believer in entropy. While his fiction deals with dislocated men, those caught on the edge of personal and cultural despair who by their sensitivity or intelligence are often pushed to the periphery of the worlds they inhabit, he refuses to confer on them the sanctification of victimhood. He is particularly persuasive when attacking the poseur of romantic despair, and his comic portrait of the code hero, Eugene Henderson, cuts the ground from under the self-appointed exile. To Bellow, the individual's life is incapable of being defined in isolation; to realize meaning, man must try to relate himself to society, to its institutions and communal values.

The view of the hero as a marginal man trying to relocate himself within the center of the community's "ordinary life," in which Bellow has implicit faith, is one frequently associated with Jewish experience and fiction. His insistence on the previousness of common life, his rejection of the beliefs that man is finished and that the world is running down have led most critics to label him a "Jewish novelist of commitment" (Howard Harper, *Desperate Faith*), a "Jewish proletariat novelist" (Chester Eisinger, *Fiction of the Forties*), or a "Jewish-American novelist" within a group currently riding the crest of public popularity (including Roth and Malamud; sometimes Mailer, Wouk, and Salinger). Bellow looks upon these labels with a mixture of amusement and disdain. When queried about the utility of the label "Jewish-American writer," he replies:

> It is accurate only insofar as it is true that I am an American and a Jew and a writer. But I don't clearly see the value of running all three of these items together. Over the years I have been faintly amused at the curious linkage of Bellow, Malamud, and Roth. Somehow it always reminds me of Hart, Shaffner, and Marx.

In a more serious vein, he adds:

> I wonder if there isn't an implied put-down in the label American-Jewish Writer. One doesn't, after all, any longer speak of American Irish Writers or American Italian Writers or, for that matter, American Wasp Writers. What's more, the label seems to me without a shred of literary accuracy, for the writers

who have had it pasted on their backs seem to me to vary tremendously: in their styles, in their subject matter and certainly in their quality.[4]

Yet when Bellow talks about Jewish writers, he also emphasizes their experience as being different from that of other American writers.

The question whether they [Jewish-American writers] had a right to this [English] language and to this literature was a lively question. In their own eyes they sometimes felt that they didn't have the right because they weren't born to the manor, and American society—at least its elite Anglo-Saxon elements—told them that they didn't come by it naturally and that it didn't really belong to them.[5]

Certainly Bellow is part of an affirmative Jewish tradition, a reflection of a culture that, as Irving Howe describes it, "does not assume evil to be the last word about man." But Bellow's work deserves equal treatment as a part of the American literary heritage in which it finds its insistence on sloughing off the old forms and trying to create new, coherent, and vital expressions of American experience.

I contend that Bellow's work is deeply rooted, intellectually and morally, within the American literary consciousness in ways that all claims of special heritage tend to obscure. I do not propose to err in the way some critics have done by pasting labels upon a codified American literary consciousness. There is no unitary character of mainstream American literature; we have become accustomed to think of it as a divided stream. Nor do I wish to weary the reader with yet another recapitulation of the American tradition. Rather, I wish to suggest that Bellow's fiction, in its own unique admixture, reflects repeating elements, preoccupations, dreams, and desires that make it American literature with a special signature.

As Jackson J. Benson suggests, the central tradition in American literature is moralistic and often allegorical. "The value system carried within this tradition has usually been broadly humanistic, rather than narrowly religious, emphasizing such concerns as the liberation of the human spirit and the need for love, faith, and respect in human relationships. As allegory, our fiction has sought to objectify the persistent spiritual conflict within the American psyche . . . such objectification by allegory may be in terms of landscape, of objects, or of other characters."[6]

Concomitant with the moral and allegorical nature of our tradition is the obsession of our primary narrative with adaptability, with change, with what Henderson calls "becoming." It sees itself as launched upon what Crevecoeur called, in a mixture of admiration and apprehension, "a new continent," which is not so much a virgin land as it is an imaginative arena in which any condition can prevail. The American writer must imagine, in terms appropriate to his or her experience, the shape of the New World as it is engaged in its continuous process of redefinition and self-assessment.

Allegorical. Moral. Protean. Not only does Bellow's work reflect each of these characteristics, but it mixes the three so thoroughly that the quests upon which the heroes are launched, the griefs they seek to assuage, the relationships they hope to repair are all suspended in the same solution. Social and political questions are really moral, even religious ones. The landscapes we create and inhabit condition who and what we become. Who we are determines what we love, which—in turn—determines what will survive deterioration and death. It is not the *presence* of these elements that American literature claims with any kind of exclusivity; it is the amalgam of the three, each present in proportion to the others.

If an artist in search of America becomes a "sort of Columbus," he does so in an effort to create meaning out of a continent as yet inadequately named. It is redefined, renamed, in the full recognition that reality extends beyond any single definition applied by other explorers. "That's the struggle of humanity," says Augie March, "to recruit others to your version of what's real." Each American artist struggles against such recruitments in order to make his own. His second struggle, equally difficult, is to avoid being seduced by his own version of the real.

Bellow's narratives reflect the transcendentalist's desire to create a new shape out of one's unique artistic consciousness and against the imprisoning shapes of the external world. The trap of this approach, as Emerson and Melville and Poe so clearly revealed, is that the self may become imprisoned in the very system it has devised. Defining the self involves the risk of confining the self.

Such definitions require rigorous self-examination, and in Bellow's novels this difficulty of discriminating accurately is compounded by an urban setting bombarding one with choices. Although retreat from society's pressures is often a necessary prelude to discovery, reentry is crucial. Although the immediate present is compelling, an awareness of the history which has formed that present is imperative. Such a symbiosis between man and his environment reflects the naturalism evident in Bellow's fiction. If we understand naturalism as defined by the central image in Crane or Dreiser of a person adrift in a sea of indifference, subject to the ebb and flow of the tide, we instantly recognize the special torment of Tommy Wilhelm, the last awful days of Humboldt, the impotence of Albert Corde in Rumania. Repeatedly Bellow's fiction asks, Can we hope for more than physical survival? Under what terms do we wish to survive? Naturalism for Bellow, unlike that in Dreiser or Crane, is not a philosophical premise. It is simply the appropriate backdrop of urban pressure against which compelling human relationships vie for attention.

Bellow's later novels, particularly *Mr. Sammler's Planet* and *The Dean's December*, wrestle with questions of culture and civilization. Their emphasis upon a central informing sensibility that tries to make sense of the past and order in the present reflects the concerns and methodology of Henry Adams and Henry James. Like Adams and James, Bellow in his most recent fiction wants to reclaim history, reassert the ideal of culture in the face of contemporary barbarism. Sammler and Corde are each a prime example of "one on whom nothing is lost." Yet in both predecessors, the judgment of the American character is made in juxtaposition to the mores of Europe. James's heroes and heroines become inverted Columbus figures, setting sail from America to discover the Old World. Bellow's *Bildungsro-*

mane work in the opposite direction, and finally, in the conclusions to *Mr. Sammler's Planet* and *The Dean's December*, he shoots the imagination off this planet and into interstellar space.

Bellow's map of the New World suggests that man ultimately negotiates his own contract with life. Faith is not a reflex action; it must be earned through the consideration of the full range of human experience and "it cannot exist without the knowledge of profound despair."[7] Augie, Henderson, Sammler, and Citrine make choices that are acts of faith within an incredibly muddled, chaotic urban environment. Yet their choices attest to neither a religious orthodoxy nor a full-blown metaphysic. For Bellow the novel comes before the philosophy, and at best, "fiction is only the jittery act of reaching."[8] But it is this jittery act that is crucial to American literature. It is, as Wallace Stevens has suggested, "The mind in the act of finding / What will suffice."

Bellow's "act of finding" also suggests important modifications in the American tradition. Unlike the Puritan settlers, who found themselves in the condition of having to create anew the terms of their identities, Bellow's heroes are second-generation European Jews with a rich history and an ancient culture. They know "who they are." They strive less to establish identity than to discover the terms through which that identity can renew itself, recover stability, and live meaningfully. At the same time, Bellow's heroes define themselves against the sharp edges of a half-alien culture. They are never wholly nor comfortably assimilated into WASP America, and their sense of themselves is forged in the realization that they are both a part of American life and apart from it.

Further, Bellow's works caution against the absolute virtues of the transcendental "eye" by suggesting the dangers in the kind of solipsism that rides on the shoulders of the American initiate as he hits the open road. In addition to resisting society's entrapments, the Bellow hero must resist those of his own formulation. And orphanhood is not a condition to be cultivated. On the contrary, Bellow's heroes are proud of their ties to a past—to, as Augie puts it, "a personal history and family enough to be loyal to." Consequently, they seek to explore the nature of human ties rather than of separations, connections rather than cleavages. Joseph observes to himself, but also to the column of lonely questers who march through American literary history, "Goodness is achieved not in a vacuum, but in the company of other men, attended by love (92)."

Perhaps more than in any other way, Bellow's work lies squarely within American literature's preoccupations in its insistence on what Augie calls "venturing as far as possible." In response to this felt need, Bellow's fiction combines the moral, allegorical, and protean impulses most clearly. Augie journeys outward to discover as much as he can; Asa and Joseph journey inward. Henderson crosses continents; Herzog traverses intellectual history; Sammler, time and space; Citrine, death and rebirth; Corde, crematoriums and astral space. They all explore to the limits of their experience and individual resources how best to "know," and in that knowledge how best to live. This is a voyage begun in the spirit of Whitman's incantatory plea, "Oh, farther, farther sail." It is a journey that bypasses any simplistic notions of political or communal salvation, utopian solutions, or romantic posturing. It insists that life is open-ended and, as yet, verdictless. In this effort Bellow continues to shape the tradition he inherits as well as reflect some of its deepest roots. Both his affirmations and his oppositions fire the American imagination with new possibilities, new ways to define itself and be free.

Bellow has been described as a great realist; a follower of Dreiser, Norris, and the American urban naturalist tradition; a great romantic, especially in the yearnings for intuitive understanding that register in *Henderson the Rain King*, *The Adventures of Augie March*, and *Seize the Day*; and as the last of the Yiddish story-spinners. Bellow's critics have been aware from the outset, it seems, of the difficulties of consigning his work to any single literary or historical context. And there is an abundance of criticism. As Leslie Field notes, three book-length bibliographies published in Belgium, Britain, and the United States by 1977 accentuated the international recognition afforded Bellow after the Nobel Prize of 1976.[9] The great outpouring of critical and scholarly work on Saul Bellow after the

Nobel award led one young Indian scholar, Chirantan Kulshrestha, to suggest that "the increasing bulk of scholarship on
Saul Bellow has begun to approach the proportions of a minor
industry." [10] Yet when *Modern Fiction Studies* devoted a special
issue to Bellow studies (Spring 1979), its detailed checklist of
criticism suggested that very few of Bellow's critics have attempted in any systematic way to see his work in the context
of a larger American literary tradition. As Leslie Field com-
plains, "There still seems to be too much parochialism, indis-
criminate parallel and source hunting, and dead-end 'pattern
probing' in Bellow criticism." [11]

I intend to examine the individual novels and their cumulative insights in the light of Jackson Benson's query: "how our
fiction has sought to objectify the persistent spiritual conflict
within the American psyche." Not only does this sort of inquiry
require placing Bellow within a cultural and intellectual frame-
work, a task of significant interest to me, but it also offers a
way of combating a recurrent and frustrating problem in presenting Bellow in the college classroom. Despite considerable
critical attention to Bellow's relationship to traditional American literature—as early as Leslie Fiedler's well-known essay,
"The Jew as Mythic American" (*Ramparts*, Autumn 1963)—
editors of standard anthologies, journalists, and literary critics
of the stature of Maxwell Geismar, Irving Howe, and Alfred
Kazin continue to speak of Bellow in terms of special cate-
gories. As a result, a student approaches Bellow's fiction with
a set of hyphenated cultural assumptions already dancing in his
or her head. It is not surprising that he or she "finds" idiosyncratic experience in stories that are listed under such labels as
"Assimilationist Dreams," "Minority Voices," "Jewish and Black
Protest." Such "discoveries" are simply exercises in self-fulfilling
prophecy. To make a convincing case for Bellow's position in
mainstream American literature is, in part, my effort toward
remedying that situation.

Following the lead of Richard Chase (*The American Novel and
Its Tradition*), Jonathan Baumbach in *The Landscape as Nightmare*
suggests that the contemporary American novel has "blood ties
with the romance." While I resist his notion that the romance

produced only the "underside of consciousness," the strategies it employs and its artistic intentions suggest the pattern for my chapter divisions. The substance of the romance contains the protean, moral, and allegorical stresses I suggested earlier. And the strategies of the romance bridge the gritty streets of the "actual" with the dreams of the "possible."

In Hawthorne's "neutral territory in which the real and the imaginary may meet, each embuing itself with the nature of the other," the world is neither actual nor dream. Vision permits the perceiver to distinguish the real from the transitory. How the hero sees is the focus of Chapter 1.

If the purpose of heightened vision is to allow the hero to create meaning, to snatch from the multiple forms and distractions of the world those values that will give order and meaning to life, then withdrawal is the first tactic. The American hero moves out from the fixities imposed by society to discover value "in exile." Reentry is the corollary step since, as Hawthorne insists, the achieving of a satisfactory identity depends on interaction, on active participation in society. Chapter 2 explores this pattern of exile and return.

Chapter 3 investigates the task of articulating meaning— through words, in relationships, in action—the process that when fixed and formulated in a phrase becomes the "lessons in the real" for Bellow's characters. Meaning in the romance, says Hawthorne, is to be glimpsed, not deduced by cold logic or abstract reasoning. Humanly significant truth is "of the heart" and is more likely to come within the receptive state Hawthorne called the "passive sensibility." While Bellow's novels never deny the purposeful grasp of directed thinking, truth more often comes through the intuitions and the heart. Bellow's heroes find truth in the responsible imagination and the fullness of personal experience.

Chapter 4 summarizes these patterns and looks at them in the paradigm of Hemingway's fiction. Ernest Hemingway's novels picture a world in which the hero, perceiving the hostility from without, withdraws in an effort to impart meaning and order to existence, and reenters bearing the imprint of his own instruction and insight. Since Hemingway's influence was at its zenith when Bellow entered the scene in 1937—44, this chapter examines in detail the Hemingway model and its temptations and limits for Bellow.

Finally, a novel cannot be discussed solely in terms of its ideation. This problem is particularly acute in a study of Bellow's work because his ideas are so persuasive and he, too, seems enamored of them. Such authorial tendencies push critics such as Leslie Fiedler into exasperation over Bellow's "desire to preach." The quality of a work's abstractable ideas is, of course, one signal of its value, but meaning comes from its total rendered experience, what James called its "felt life." How the "felt life" of a Bellow novel generates its own unique truth is the focus of the last chapter. In it I examine both Bellow's success in transcending his own ideation and his recent difficulty in avoiding authorial instruction.

Bellow's style, his literary aesthetic, is his means of combining the allegorical patterns and the individual freedoms that relate him to and release him from the previously existing forms of American literature. As Richard Poirer has argued in *A World Elsewhere*, language itself provides a kind of verbal space between solipsism and social systems. Bellow's special gift is the creation and enrichment of this verbal space. His is a style that incorporates the transcendental "eye" while still remaining conscious of its seductions, that creates the pressure of urban sprawl without implying naturalistic causation, that honors "grace under pressure" without capitulating to its flip side: suicide. In short, it articulates the American milieu, which has shaped it and which it also seeks to challenge.

In this insistence, Bellow is most like his recent protagonist, Albert Corde, forever picking up signals from "all over the universe":

> "He looked out, noticing. What a man he was for noticing! Continually attentive to his surroundings. As if he had been sent down to *mind* the outer world, on a mission of observation and notation. The object of which was? To link up? To classify? To penetrate?" (*Dean's December*, 210).

Sammler is "a delicate recording instrument." Herzog is "a prisoner of perception; a compulsory witness." As in Poe's *Nar-*

rative of Arthur Gordon Pym, Hawthorne's *Scarlet Letter*, and Melville's *Moby-Dick*, man is pictured as (the ultimate) explorer of internal and external space. He is also the reader of hieroglyphics, the supervisor of the customhouse, the sub-sublibrarian—the dedicated and tireless translator of the signs by which he lives. As I see it, Bellow's greatest stress is on vision, on the ways in which environment conditions vision and vision transcends environment. This reciprocity registers within the sensibility of a new American hero. His "complex fate" is to translate the signs by which he lives, keenly conscious of the intersecting planes of time, place, and history.

Chapter One

The Health of the Eye

"The health of the eye demands a horizon."
Emerson

*I*n 1941 Saul Bellow published his first story, "Two Morning Monologues," in *Partisan Review*. Both monologues, which together constitute the story, investigate the ways in which man looks at his experience, the ways in which he processes the contradictions he sees in that experience. Each story concentrates on the function of the perceiver, the "I" through whom information is received, processed, ordered, and evaluated. In so doing, the stories serve as useful introductions to Bellow's general vision and define two poles of response between which later heroes vacillate.

The first monologue is narrated by a bright young man, an intellectual who can't get a job after five years of college training. Like Joseph, the hero of Bellow's first novel, *Dangling Man*, he is waiting for his draft call and meanwhile fills his time with aimless activity. He feels closeted at home and is capable only of peering at the world from within his own experience. He admits sadly that "the chief difficulty is in disposing of the day."[1] Yet there seems little hope of change or getting out. The narrator has acquiesced to his cage, assumed the terms of his condition to be fixed, and pronounced his state as "sunk." "I know a great deal about myself," he says, "in as well as out—privately, that is, as well as statistically. I'm very nearly sunk. What sort of getting away would that be? Total it any way, top to bottom, reverse the order, it makes no difference, the sum is always sunk" (231). The point of view in the story, then, is one which is the expression of a condition rather than an identity, a fact underscored by the subtitle of the monologue, "Without Work."

The second monologue is spoken by a horseplayer who is also questioning his place in the "system," the order inherent in his experience, and his capacity to control that experience. He argues that man creates his own condition by finding a way to take advantage of the system, to shape that system to his own desired ends. "There's a way through the cracks," he says. "This city, this country is full of them and it's up to people like me to find a way through them." The game is not easy, but "win or lose, you call the shots. . . . It's in your hands and in your power" (235). Significantly, the subtitle "The Gambler" suggests both an identity and an activity, since the gambler's betting is an attempt to assert his individuality through his own free choice.

The behavior of Bellow's two narrators—aimless drifting by the one and continuous directed action by the other—underscores special problems of vision and the visionary, the "eye/I," which have been under investigation by American authors since they first began describing man's introduction to this continent. The problems of identity that "Two Morning Monologues" describes involve what Emerson called "a horizon." That horizon derives from man's way of perceiving his experience, and it involves the search to find a self, a form that orders life and gives it meaning. No movement was more devoted to investigating the health of the eye and its horizons than transcendentalism, growing as it did from European philosophy and speculation rooted in German romanticism and French rationality. Set against a background of America as model, as the Puritans' "Errand in the Wilderness," Emerson's insistence on the poet as seer, Melville's concept of the artist as maker, and Whitman's notions of the artist as mystical namer pushed the exploration of the perceiver and the perceiver's consciousness into the forefront of the American literary consciousness. The investigations resulting from this interest proceeded from two differing assumptions. Emerson assumed that there was a divine plan inherent in the universe, which, while perhaps not accessible to man in his given lifetime, was ultimately discoverable through faith and reason. If man sees only evil and pain, Emerson argued, his perception is merely partial; he fails to perceive "the whole," that total "horizon" on which the health of the eye depends. The world is ordered in logical and consistent ways, whether or not man is capable of seeing that linkage at any given time. If man assumes himself to be a victim, as does Bellow's first monologist, his assumptions about his condition are predicated on an understanding of a world ordered in predictable ways, operating by consistent laws. That he finds himself "sunk" may indicate that he sees as yet an incomplete version of his destiny; yet that destiny is discoverable. Man can reason out his place in the scheme of things.

An opposing set of assumptions grew out of Melville's insistence that the world is an enigma in which every condition of being stands as paradox to every other. There is no logical pattern in universal structures called "nature," nor is there logic in structures of human relationships called "society": "Nature is not so much her own ever-sweet interpreter, as the mere supplier of that cunning alphabet, whereby selecting and combining as he pleases, each man reads his own peculiar mind and mood" (*Pierre*). Like Bellow's gambler, Melville contends that man must devise an order for himself and *will* it to meaning. Man must attempt to control his world, all the time recognizing it as an irrational world of flux, of mysterious force and counterforce.

On these two positions swing a number of complicated questions: Can man proceed on the basis of a knowable order in the universe, or are reason and faith destined to prove inadequate in man's pursuit of truth? Is man "self-reliant," or does he need a "usable past" to fix the terms of his identity? Does meaning emerge when man withdraws from society, or it is dependent on full social engagement? These questions underlie many of the most vital dilemmas in American literature. They endeavor to place the American literary hero somewhere between reason and intuitive insight, between independence and recognition of a past of which he is a part, between the American exaltation of pioneer status and an outcast's sense of isolation from a cultural home. Bellow's work gives full play to many of these dilemmas. In *Dangling Man*, *The Victim*, and particularly *Augie March*, Bellow explores the possibilities of discovering a meaning posited in the universe and accessible to man through right thinking and right action. Joseph, of *Dangling Man*, withdraws to the solitude of his journal in hope of some discoverable insight. Reason and unreason contend within his written entries. Asa, of *The Victim*, expects history to make sense if only he can identify his place in it. Augie March's journey is an attempt to "discover the axial lines" by which man can live his life meaningfully. His discoveries suggest that the intellect alone cannot fathom the depths of man's being.

Seize the Day, Henderson, Herzog, Sammler, Humboldt's Gift, The Dean's December suggest that man is as much the maker of his destiny as he is the recipient of a logical or intuitive insight; their protagonists seek a destiny—both a gift and a responsibility—that requires rigorous self-scrutiny and critical choices. Eugene Henderson learns from King Dahfu that "you must invent your own experience," that you must cease expending energy on processes of "becoming" and instead activate your life in the present. When Tommy Wilhelm finds that an "imposter soul" has been running his life, he rejects its bogus values to "seize the day." While Herzog fights the Christian view of history that insists on "some corruption or evil to be saved from," he still tries to save himself. He believes that man creates his own destiny, but only after he understands the terms of his own history, his own mental and emotional roots. Artur Sammler identifies the source of his daughter's, his cousin's, and his students' dilemmas as their "failure to find coherence." As a Bloomsbury intellectual and Polish Jew, he is tied indisputably to European traditions, practiced in models for conduct, for logical argumentation, and for intellectual synthesis. Yet when faced with the jumbled, violent, and sometimes mad urban chaos of his immediate surroundings, he concludes that logical structures alone cannot explain man to himself. To "know what one knows" is a spontaneous and intuitive act, an act one wills to meaning. Despite Charles Citrine's assertion that "conditions were very tough," the world itself contains what he needs to know to bring order and meaning to life. While Albert Corde participates in a death watch over his wife's mother, over the death of the cities, over the death of morality, he continues to believe that "the first act of morality was to disinter the reality, retrieve reality, dig it out from the trash, represent it anew."

It is possible, then, to see Bellow's work as portraying heroes stretching between reason and unreason, autonomy and history, withdrawal and social engagement. Each need is a privately felt need, even if it has its parallel underpinnings in American literary history and in the growing sense that it is, as Henry James maintained, a "complex fate" to be an American. Bellow uses the tradition quite self-consciously, particularly in his two panoramic picaresques, *The Adventures of Augie March* and *Henderson the Rain King*. Augie is an Emersonian man ("you want there should be Man, with capital M, with great stature")[2] who finds all the great men to be sadly lacking. Like Huck Finn, whose "adventures" and beliefs in "a better fate" he parallels, Augie lights out for the Territory only to discover that it holds no more clues for him than the present. His adventures take him on a journey through American literary history where passage after passage echoes the stance that earlier American writers assumed in matters of identity and personal destiny. Echoing Whitman, Augie says that in questions of "parentage, and other history," he will go on "assuming about others what I assumed about myself" (147). When he observes cattle grazing on a peaceful hillside, he rhapsodizes in Thoreauvian style about "mere creatures [who] look with their original eyes" (330). His brother, Simon, is a cross between Clyde Griffith and Jay Gatsby when he announces his marriage to a prominent socialite in the confident tones of one who thinks he has realized the American Dream: "Well sport, we may be married in the next few months. You envy me? I bet you do" (150).

If *Augie March* sounds like American literary history on parade, *Henderson the Rain King* is the story of a man who has passed the reviewing stand once too often. Eugene Henderson is an aging American picaro, remarkable for his size, his sensitivity, and his capacity for failure. In addition to the obvious satiric parallels to the Hemingway code hero's doctrine of der- ring-do, the book is also filled with echoes from the pages of American literary history. At one point Henderson is transfixed by an octopus that seems to be consuming itself and whose tentacles appear to beckon to him. It is a passage shockingly reminiscent of the octopus-squid survival battle waged in Dreiser's consciousness—the battle of naturalistic determin- ism. Further on in his redemptive search, when Henderson feels his "old self" resisting, incapable of relating to the lion, he confesses to Dahfu: "It's got a terrific grip on me. . . . As if I were carrying an eight-hundred-pound load—like a Galápa- gos turtle. On my back."[3] The reference to the turtles of Mel- ville's *Encantadas*, that search to the ends of the cinder and lava wastelands of the earth, is a part of Henderson's "lessons in reality." Finally, at the close of the novel, when Henderson meets the orphan on the return plane to America, he claims, "I am an Ishmael, too" (338), suggesting that within his insights and limitations he has lived out a tale that he has returned to tell.

To read Bellow's literature is to walk down a road marked by familiar signposts. Yet, Bellow's work is not simply a re- arrangement of prior positions, a new orchestration of themes originally composed by Emerson, Whitman, Melville, Twain, James, Dreiser, Hemingway. Bellow's treatment of these themes points to two things: (1) their continuing impact and applica- bility, and (2) the inadequacy of any single position to explore and express fully the dilemma of modern man in America. In *Augie March* and *Henderson* particularly, Bellow seems to be moving his hero beyond the questions and answers generated by Melville's philosophic despair, Dreiser's determinism, Hem- ingway's separate peace. Augie's and Henderson's quests are about them, but finally not of them. There are other truths to be examined; man has a firm basis neither for affirmation nor for denial as yet.

Bellow's fiction absorbs and reflects, with obsessive concern, a trend best described as the relationship between experience and identity, the relationship between what is seen and who is seeing. Frequently Bellow explores within a single novel the possibility of the hero as "seer" *and* "maker" of his own experience. Since such a close relationship exists between the seer and the seen, the maker and the values he generates, the health of the "eye" is also an important investigation into the health of the "I." Man's sense of identity hinges on what he perceives as valuable.

The two impulses interpenetrate in *Dangling Man*, when Joseph, awaiting his draft induction notice, begins a journal, a "record of inward transactions," which he intends as an exercise in self-definition. The period is one of increasing alienation, frustration, and frantic internal dialogue. Seeing himself as a "moral casualty of the war," he at first juxtaposes inner and outer realities in his life to locate the kinds of correspondences that Emerson suggested were the fabric of the universe. Joseph tries, in vain, to envision a correlation between exterior life and interior life, between the billboards and culverts outside his boardinghouse window and the signs and signals within his private existence. His intention is to establish both as an order in "nature" and, by extension, in "society."

> I could see a long way from this third floor height. Not far off there were chimneys, their smoke a lighter gray than the gray of the sky; and, straight before me, ranges of poor dwellings, warehouses, billboards, culverts, electric signs blankly burning, parked cars and moving cars, and the occasional bare plan of a tree. There I surveyed, pressing my forehead on the glass. It was my painful obligation to look and to submit to myself the invariable question: Where was there a particle of what, elsewhere, or in the past, had spoken in man's favor? There could be no doubt that these billboards, streets, tracks, houses, ugly and blind, were related to interior life. And yet, I told myself, there had to be a doubt. There were human lives organized around these ways and houses, and that they, the houses say, were the analogue, that what men created they also were, through some transcendent means, I could not bring myself to concede. . . . The worlds we bargained for were never the worlds we got.[4]

Although the theory of correspondence fails, Joseph continues to believe in the possibility that meaning is discoverable if only he can know himself, detach himself from the distractions of the immediate present, and climb into his own pure perception of the world. As he says of himself, "he is keenly intent on knowing what is happening to him. He wants to miss nothing" (27). In trying to be one "on whom nothing is lost," Joseph chronicles in his journal compulsive concern with personal freedom, individual perception, and free choice. Not surprisingly, his conversations with himself and his alter ego become more confining and claustrophobic than the empty social lives of the friends he castigates. While he is contemptuous of the "Ideal Constructions" of the past, he continues "some sort of personal effort" to locate "exclusive focus, passionate and engulfing," which will catapult his life into meaning. Instead, he finds the burden of his freedom dreadful and decides to dissolve his isolation by fiat; he submits to impersonal authority by volunteering for the army. He still clings to the faint promise of discovering a self or a pattern that orders life and gives it meaning: "Perhaps the war could teach me, by violence, what I had been unable to learn during those months in the room. Perhaps I could sound creation through other means. Perhaps" (191). Yet he recognizes that introspection is not enough. "The next move was the world's. I could not bring myself to regret it." For Joseph, to be "man thinking" is an intolerable burden, and finally more constricting than it is liberating.

Clearly, in *Dangling Man* the problem of discovering meaning in life is inextricably tied to the identity of the "seer." The vision bears the imprint of the visionary, and Joseph's attempt to discover meaning hinges on his awareness of his true self, the separation of that "self" from what Emerson called "mean egotism." A part of Joseph's problem is his inability to make that separation. He is contemptuous of friends, neighbors, relatives, his old self, his present self—indeed, he has no trustworthy mirror in which to check "correspondences." All he has is the broken and discarded shards of a past he disclaims. There is little possibility of discovery and less of invention in a figure who perceives his own outlines so dimly. "The health of the eye demands a horizon," Emerson counseled, and Joseph possesses no points of reference outside himself. He can only watch himself watching himself.

Asa Leventhal in *The Victim* also confronts the mirror of identity and comes to know who he is precisely by learning who he is not. As a Jew, Asa feels himself an outsider at the trade magazine where he works. He senses that he got his job through "pull," has married his wife through a lucky reversal in her attitude, and feels as if the order of his life has been dictated by chance, which could alter itself at any moment. Asa's inability to know who he is and how he relates to others hinges on his feeling that he does not deserve the position he holds. His fears are those of a man riding on the circumference of the wheel of fortune, awaiting the hand at the hub to turn. Kirby Allbee materializes as that hand. A member of a prominent New England family, Allbee blames his ruin on the displacement of his class by the Jews and believes Leventhal is the particular Jew who deposed him. "The world's changed hands," he says. "I'm like the Indian who sees a train running over the prairie where the buffalo used to roam."[5] This novel stresses not only the problems of individual perception of the world, but the world's coercions on the perceiver. Asa's problems hinge on his relationship to an American past, a heritage that he feels estranged from as a Jew. Allbee's feeling that he is dispossessed, that his place in American history has been usurped by the Leventhals of this world, fuels his accusations as surely as personal guilt. Unlike Joseph, who in large measure willed his isolation, Asa and Allbee are not willfully displaced persons; they find themselves dislocated in a world where old notions of order have been upset. This dislocation generates fear; fear generates defenses, guilt projections, paranoia; and the book becomes a study both of how society victimizes men and of how men victimize one another.

Since Allbee decides Asa is "entirely to blame" for the death of his wife as well as the failure of his career, he decides to make him accountable by invading Asa's previously secure existence. He comes to live at his apartment, reads his intimate mail, sleeps with a whore in Asa's marriage bed, and uses his oven for a suicide attempt. He is allowed these encroachments because of Asa's confused guilt and flagging will—indeed, because of Asa's dangerous passivity. His usurpation of Asa's life points up the escape clause implicit in victimhood: to consider oneself a victim is to abdicate responsibility for one's life. While Asa needs to think of himself as a victim, he is continually outvictimed by Allbee. Each claims he is the prey of the other. In fact, the two become mirrors of one another; the interlocking of the two lives underscores the fact that guilt and persecution weld lives together.[6] Asa and Allbee's final death struggle is, appropriately enough for a study of anti-Semitism, at the oven when Asa finally splits their twinhood by refusing to be either victim or victimizer, murdered or murderer; Asa will not "be gassed," and in this determination he begins to unravel the complications of guilt and expiation that have bound his identity to Allbee's. Since he opts for life, one which will lead to some sense of connection with his fellowman, he must reject Allbee's fateful *doppelgänger* game; if he does not, he will, like Poe's William Wilson, succeed only in slaying himself.

Although Asa's struggle with "seeing" the true terms of his life is most frequently confined to his twinship with Allbee, he does have other points of reference outside his own private experience. Both the concern he demonstrates for his brother's family in their moments of crisis and the valuable instruction he receives from friends, particularly the patriarch Schlossberg, underscore the fundamental worth of life and the possibilities of genuine self-regard. The only meaning in life is what we give it, Schlossberg says, so "why be measly? . . . Choose dignity. Nobody knows enough to turn it down" (134). To know where you are going, Schlossberg counsels, you must know where you came from. He insists that the old Jewish custom of sewing one's own shroud was a good one because "at least they knew where they stood and who they were, in those days" (255). Modern man has fewer points of reference, and veils those he has. At funerals today, Schlossberg says, there is paper grass to hide the dust to which we all return, and "paper grass in the grave makes all the grass paper" (256). Human worth, Asa discovers through his contacts with family and friends, is a quality of life dependent on acknowledging who you are as well as who you are not.

In a world where contingency is an undeniable fact—where, as Allbee says, "'if' swings us around by the ears like rabbits"(202)—man is still confronted with choices that hinge on his wholeness of self. Definition of that self is hard in a world where all the choices are disguised. But there is the possibility of choosing dignity. Even Allbee acknowledges this dimension when he says, "I know what really goes on inside me . . . there isn't a man who doesn't. All this business, 'Know thyself!' Everybody knows but nobody wants to admit it" (226–27). Asa comes to "admit" the terms of his true life, but whether or not he can act on it is a question the book leaves open.

Augie March has no difficulty in *acting*. He acts and acts and acts in an effort to discover what principles may inform those actions. While Augie still hopes to discover "axial lines," his concern is not so much with how that discovery mirrors his own identity; rather, he hopes it will guide his actions, render them meaningful and purposeful. Discovery is not a means of explaining Augie to himself but rather a means of activating a life of self-regard in the face of collective power and authority.

Augie sees the problem of the subjective self quite early. Although a prime adoptee for diverse characters, he resists being appropriated into others' "versions of the real." That leads him to ask what the self becomes if unreinforced by systematized ways of perceiving and acting. His energy, his inclusiveness, and his powers of evasion allow him to escape from the mirrored self that paralyzes Joseph and frustrates Asa. In racing Augie past numbers of persons, each of whom has created a version of the world that orders reality and supports his view of himself, Bellow is deliberately mocking Einhorn, Magnus, Renling, and other characters who try to fit reality into their version of "how it is." Augie, in his rejection of these dicta, becomes a master avoider, an elusive runner who lights out for new territory every time he feels the halter of a new version around his neck. He exercises avoidance rather than freedom, for true independence lies in knowing, in deeply satisfying ways, specifically *why* and *what* one is rejecting. In scanning the horizon for future possibilities, Augie sacrifices the short view. He shucks off teachers simply to celebrate unencumbrance, but seems to have only the vaguest promptings of what he endorses. Augie continues to believe that one can identify his own "horizon," but only when striving stops can the axial lines emerge. "I have trouble being still, and . . . my hope is based upon getting to be still so that the axial lines can be found" (*Augie March*, 514). For Augie, "a man's character is his fate . . . and in the end there isn't any way to disguise the nature of the knocks by acoustical work on the door or gloving the knuckles" (3). Augie tries to chronicle this character and, in knowing it through its actions, discover how to navigate life. But for all the independence of his tone, he seldom *initiates* any course of action, seldom makes a creative choice; and when he does "discover," he fails to act upon that discovery. Like the eagle who hovers over the plain, he can see the paths of the creatures below. But when he does make his pounce, he disappoints. Fascinated by life's possibilities, Augie refuses to alight and hold. He remains the avoider even in the teeth of the realization that man must confront.

The problems, then, of Bellow's first three novels hinge on the hero's attempts to separate himself from his environment. He wishes to investigate the terms of his own private self; simultaneously he is forced to acknowledge the real relationship existing between that self and its past, its personal history, and the social circumstances in which that self exists. The "eye" and the "horizon" are in reciprocal relationship. Divested of Emerson's harmonious plan in which the universe is grooved to run, "Know thyself!" becomes a terrifying and complicated command for modern man, one that leads to all kinds of evasions, defenses, and projections. Still, Bellow is not willing to cancel out the value of discovery, the function of the seer in sighting the landmarks of his own life; it remains as a promissory note just out of the grasp of Joseph's subjectivity, Asa's paranoia, and Augie's evasion:

> It takes some of us a long time to find out what the price is of being in nature, and what the facts are about your tenure. How long it takes depends on how swiftly the social sugars dissolve. But when at last they do dissolve there's a different taste in your mouth, bringing different news which registers with dark astonishment and fills your eyes. And this different news is that from vast existence in some way you rise up and at any moment you

may go back. Any moment; the very next, maybe (*Augie March*, 362).

This different news which may rise at any moment can be received only when the constrictions of "mean ego" have been shucked, when the "social sugars" that coat man's ability to discriminate dissolve, and when man confronts rather than avoids. Tommy Wilhelm confronts because he is cornered, unable to run or hide elsewhere, and *Seize the Day* concentrates on a shucking off of what Tamkin calls the "imposter soul" in a single day of reckoning. Wilhelm is a man who, while trying to leap all the obstacles to fantastic American success, has hit the tops of all the hurdles: an ex-actor, unemployed, going to seed, eating too much, relying on pills, trying to keep up appearances but aware that his meaningless routine is breaking up and that "a huge trouble long presaged but till now formless was due."[7]

Tommy is obviously a sick man. His actions display a state of nervous tension continually bordering on hysteria, and he is encouraged in his self-laceration by his father's continuing indifference and his wife's demanding selfishness. But if he is sick, he is also, like Asa and Augie, able to spot the horizon which may bring health to the eye. He achieves a healing insight at the conclusion of the novella, for he passes beneath self-pity to "the source of all tears," and then "deeper than sorrow" to a center beyond grief, "the heart's ultimate need," where "the waters of the earth roll over him" (118). The drowning imagery contains both the forces that destroy the heavy corporeal self and a transcendent reality that raises the true self above destruction.[8] In an elaborate baptism metaphor reminiscent of Melville or Poe, Tommy loses his "imposter soul" in the waters of the earth preparatory to being reborn into meaningful life. Of course Tommy is not Melville's Ishmael, bobbing to the surface on the coffin of a soulmate; nor does he escape like Poe's Pym as a consequence of an accident of nature. Tommy's coffinlike buoy contains the corpse of a stranger, and whatever message is preserved as a legacy to the world is simply suggested in the emotional impact of the final scene of the novella.

Tommy is released from the bondage of his voyage. He has ceased trying to test himself against the images of expectation provided by his wife, father, children, himself. He discards the imposter soul and in its place discovers a core self free from ego-striving and false pride. In this way Tommy uncovers something "transpersonal,"[9] his human linkage to his fellow-man. That recovery allows him both to keep faith with the value of the individual self and still to link himself spiritually to others.

The ending of *Seize the Day* is blurred, emotional beyond exactness of statement; yet it appears that redemption lies within the heart's "felt need," outside the claims of the rational mind. The inadequacy of rationality as experienced by Ishmael and Pym converts to useless "ideal constructions" in *Dangling Man* and *Seize the Day*. Tommy's freedom lies in confronting what he is not, somewhat as a sculptor reveals an image by removing pieces of stone from a block. The shape of Tommy's future is left unclear; his discovery of self is emotionally vague.

Eugene Henderson goes a long way toward chipping out the significant moral outlines of his existence. Henderson's journey from "I want" to "they want" is an attempt to break out of monologue into dialogue. He accomplishes this by confronting something larger than the self (the lion), something that terminates the self (death), something that controls the self (love). Henderson's journey is begun out of a drive for discovery, but it ends in the recognition that man must invent his own experience and will it to meaning. His journey is more than a private quest; he is equipped with enough American-innocent-abroad trappings to suggest that he is a rotund representative of America. Like Melville's prototypical American innocent, Captain Delano, Henderson leaps to redeem situations he totally misapprehends. In blowing the cistern that contains the water supply for a whole tribe, in rising to move the giant statue of Mummah and inadvertently making himself a captive Rain King, Henderson learns the dangers of the missionary spirit. Henderson finds ways of quelling anxiety, of confronting death, of ceasing acquisitive striving; only in learning of his limits does he come to know his considerable capacities.

Henderson's quest collects the insights of prior heroes and moves beyond them. Like Joseph's quest, it is for freedom. Like Asa's, it is for worthiness. Like Augie's, it is for axial lines. Like Wilhelm's, it is for redemption. But beyond them all, it is for receptivity. Man does not process reality, Henderson learns; reality first processes man. Experience is; and it is neither beneficent nor malignant, the basis for neither hope nor despair. Man must receive it in evenness, and only then can he arrange it into meaning. Joseph, Asa, Augie, and Wilhelm are all engaged in reaching out from self-sufficient fixity. Their postures in the world are vertical—that is, assertive, egoistic, managerial. Henderson's search, though it begins in the same way, is gradually transformed into a horizontal posture—one in concert with other forms of creation, one equal with death, with sleep, with evenness. Henderson decides he will cast his lot with "being" rather than "becoming," evenness rather than striving, experience rather than schemata. He does so out of the recognition that reason alone is insufficient to explain the depths of man's being. There are other truths more mysterious to be apprehended. They can be realized only in a spontaneous and intuitive way, by opening oneself to the vibrations of Africa, by "lying on the skin of a drum." [10]

If receptivity is the keystone of Henderson's quest, the major portion of the novel traces a series of steps preparatory to achieving a state of receptivity: Henderson learns that he must move outside of all previously conditioned ways of acting; he must be purified (he is baptized in rain, mud, cow dung, leaves, sand); through the removal of the body of the dead Sungo as well as the death of Dahfu, he must learn to confront and accept death. Only by passing through these stages of initiation can he achieve a state characterized by evenness, by a cessation of striving. By consigning himself repeatedly to situations in which he is powerless, man discovers that "nothing is to be done." The ego cannot manage natural calamity, death, life. By realizing this, man is freed from pointless anxiety. Man can live, as Dahfu does, with joy even in the presence of death. Henderson's gift of life is a release from the cycle of despair; when one sees that he no longer controls life, then he has nothing in-

vested, in terms of power, to lose. This is the lesson of the dead
Sungo, the lesson of Grun-tu-molani ("man want to live!"),
and the lesson of the lion:

> You ask, what can she do for you? Many things. First she is un-
> avoidable. Test it, and you will find she is unavoidable. And this
> is what you need, as you are an avoider. . . . She will make con-
> sciousness to shine. She will burnish you. She will force the pres-
> ent moment upon you. Second, lions are experiencers. But not
> in haste. They experience with deliberate luxury. . . . She do not
> breathe shallow (260).

Henderson learns these lessons well, and while Dahfu lives, he
grows in understanding their applicability. When Dahfu is
killed, however, and Henderson is set on his own again with
his guide Romilayu, his old self returns to doubt, looking for
some ultimate justification. He cries:

> "Between the beginning and the end, is it promised?"
> "Whut promise, sah?"
> "Well, I mean something *clear*. Isn't it promised? Romilayu, I
> suppose I mean the reason—*the* reason. It may be postponed
> until the last breath. But there is justice. I believe there is justice,
> and that much is promised. Though I am not what I thought"
> (328).

Whether or not Henderson is capable of sustaining his state of
evenness without submersion into the old rage, the striving,
the need for notions of personal equity, is a question the novel
stops short of answering. Bellow leaves us with the willingness
to believe he can sustain his African insights, for Henderson
carries with him the lion cub representative of Dahfu's spirit.
Adopting the orphan on the plane, he decides, "Once more.
Whatever gains I ever made were always due to love and nothing else" (339). Yet the novel's persuasive force rests in its
questions rather than its answers.

Moses Herzog, Artur Sammler, Charles Citrine, and Albert
Corde become articulators of some of the most significant moral
questions Bellow's work explores. Herzog's method of inquiry
is one of frantic mental dialectic racing between the need to

retreat and the need to act; the need to support individual conscience and the need to obey the law; the desire to right the past and the need to live in the present; the duties demanded by the self and the obligations owed to others. Stretched taut between the claims of each of these pairs of forces, Herzog finds it is insufficient to develop a negative capability, embracing two contradictory ideas and celebrating the fullness of their opposition; this leads only to a paralysis. Instead, Herzog finds that to act, to cope with the reality of these opposing claims, he must develop the stance Fitzgerald described in "The Crack-Up": "The test of a first-rate intelligence is the ability to hold two opposed ideas in the mind at the same time, and *still retain the ability to function.*" It is this ability to function that becomes the hub of the wheel for Herzog, and the novel circles back upon itself, announcing a new start on legitimate work. Man is not freed from his character; he simply discovers the true terms of that character, and in so doing he is freed from the claims of the "imposter soul." The cyclical pattern is one that moves from method, which is determined, to meaning, which is chosen. In the process man does learn, and what he learns is best summarized in the aphorisms at the beginning and ending of *Augie March*. In that novel, "man's character is his fate" is transposed into "man's fate is his character." In the first instance, man's character implies a genetic and environmental Skinnerian box, whose "input" method is fixed and whose "output" determines man's destiny. In the second instance, man's destiny, his meaning, is open to whatever he discovers the true terms of his character to be. His character is funnel-shaped, open-ended, and within that freedom Herzog finds the peace of coexistence with the rats and birds of his Berkshire retreat. In this emphasis Bellow suggests that transcendence comes not from some outside nature writ large, nor from dissolving into the One, but rather from the "infinitude of the private man" (Emerson).

Herzog's freedom is a cumulative insight, one that is signposted in American literature's explorations. Emerson announces that "the individual is the world" (*Self-Reliance*, 1832); Thoreau adds, "Be a Columbus to whole new continents and worlds within you, opening new channels, not of trade but of thought" (*Walden*, 1854); Whitman announces, "At the end of the open road / man finds himself" (*Leaves of Grass*, 1855). Herzog, in a variety of ways, is the inheritor of this mantle of the American quester, the figure of vast potentiality poised at the start of a new history in a world offering humanity a second chance. Herzog is a tarnished version (an aging sensualist, a failure at marriage and at fulfilling his early academic promise), and humanity's second chance is portrayed in a tangled web of menacing and hostile experience; nevertheless, Herzog challenges himself to use his imperfection as a means of promoting growth, both in "the short view" as he surveys his own life, and in the "horizon view" as he notes his relationship to his history and to his fellowmen in the present. It is particularly his personal growth that is chronicled in the novel and marks an advance from the "rebirth" of Eugene Henderson. One remembers that Henderson insisted, despite his lessons from Dahfu, that justice must exist. Herzog's point of departure rests on an inquiry into the nature of justice.

He puts the question of justice early in the novel when he inquires "whether justice on this earth can or cannot be general, social, but must originate within each heart" (219). He is divided in his answer to this question, for when he writes to Eisenhower, he tells him that "to Tolstoi, freedom is entirely personal. That man is free whose condition is simple, truthful—real." But he also tells Eisenhower about Hegel, who "understood the essence of human life to be derived from history. History, memory—that is what makes us human, that, and our knowledge of death."[11] Herzog's struggle, his need to "explain, to have it out, to justify, to put in perspective, to clarify, to make amends," (2) is the record of the coexistence of these two *gestalten*. Consequently, Herzog is faced with the need to acknowledge his past, a past that includes indisputable ties to European traditions, ways of thinking, and intellectual models for shaping conduct, while simultaneously celebrating his own independence and unique self.

Herzog's struggle with notions of personal equity and with his place in human history constitutes the narrative of the novel. But the novel is less a record of what Herzog does than it is of the accumulation of circumstance, error, conflict, paradox that registers as an individual lives it. Once again Bellow's fiction begins at the point of greatest density, the peak of pressure in a man's life. His heroes are burdened men who discover that they must avoid being engulfed by their burdens while still recognizing them as essential components of their identities. "We must be what we are. That is necessary" (66). It is this attempted balance that Herzog embraces in ordering his life at the Berkshire retreat: "You gave me good value for my money when you explained that neuroses might be graded by the inability to tolerate ambiguous situations," he writes to his psychiatrist. "Allow me modestly to claim that I am much better now at ambiguities" (304). Unlike Melville's Pierre, Herzog does not self-destruct. Unlike Fitzgerald's persona in "The Crack-Up," he does not "crack like a plate." He accommodates and lives, not as a "marvelous Herzog" but as one "pretty well satisfied to be" (340).

Mr. Sammler's Planet is Bellow's fullest treatment of how man functions in the full recognition of his personal and social history. Artur Sammler, an aging journalist with Oxonian manners, an escapee from a Polish ghetto who has literally "seen beyond the grave," and this generation's father confessor, mentally records the movement of his "planet" throughout several weeks of his life in the chaotic and dangerous streets of New York's upper West Side. He is attentive to everything. He brings the same curiosity and disinterestedness to the activities of a black pickpocket observed in an uptown bus as to the details of his niece Angela's sex life; to his daughter's lunacy as to the extraordinary theories of Dr. Lal on the use we are to make of the moon now that we have reached it. "Are we to blow this great blue, white, and green planet or be blown from it?" Sammler asks dispassionately. In the record of his asking, Sammler mediates between faith and the feeling that man is powerless. He notes the law of entropy at work on this planet and sees evidence of civilized life's imminent collapse everywhere:

> Like many people who had seen the world collapse once, Mr. Sammler entertained the possibility it might collapse twice. He did not agree with refugee friends that this doom was inevitable,

but liberal beliefs did not seem capable of self-defense, and you could smell decay. You could see the suicidal impulses of civilization pushing strongly. You wondered whether this Western culture could survive universal dissemination—whether only its science and technology or administrative practices would travel, be adopted by other societies. Or whether the worst enemies of civilization might not prove to be its petted intellectuals who attacked it at its weakest moments—attacked it in the name of reason, and in the name of irrationality, in the name of visceral depth, in the name of sex, in the name of perfect instantaneous freedom. For what it amounted to was limitless demand—insatiability, refusal of the doomed creature (death being sure and final) to go away from the earth unsatisfied. A full bill of demand and complaint was therefore presented by each individual.[12]

But this record of insatiable demand and diminishing supply does not preclude Sammler's sense of flight, lightness, lift-off—the hope of a future planet. "The powers that had made the earth too small could free us from confinement. . . . So conceivably there was no alternative but to push further in the same direction, to wait for a neglected force, left in the rear, to fly forward again and recover ascendancy" (54). What, in the novel, does "fly forward again to recover ascendancy" is not the technological triumph of the moonshot, but rather man's individual capacity to care about his fellowman in the present: this capacity is documented in Sammler's daughter's pathetic theft of Dr. Lal's manuscript for her father's "edification"; in Margotte's awkward but well-intentioned attempts to keep house for Sammler; and in Sammler's special "contract" with his benefactor, Elya Gruner, a relative who had secured Sammler's release from Poland along with his daughter and who is dying from an aneurysm in the brain. As Sammler says, "When you know what pain is, you agree that not to have been born is better. *But being born, one respects the powers of creation*" (220).

Like Emerson's, the health of Sammler's "eye" depends upon its receptivity, its powers of vision, its intuitive insight: "It is something that has to go on and we all know it. The spirit feels cheated, outraged, defiled, corrupted, fragmented, injured. Still it knows what it knows, and knowledge cannot be gotten rid

of. The spirit knows that its growth is the real aim of existence"
(236).

Like Melville's, Sammler's "explanation stresses paradox," the
ambiguity that arises when "all is not flatly knowable," the
pain of suspension between yea and nay:

> The contradictions are so painful. No concern for justice? Noth-
> ing of pity? Is God only the gossip of the living? Then we
> watch these living speed like birds over the surface of a water,
> and one will dive or plunge but not come up again and never be
> seen anymore. And in our turn we will never be seen again,
> once gone through that surface. But then we have no proof that
> there is no depth under the surface. We cannot even say that our
> knowledge of death is shallow. There is no knowledge. These
> come from need, affection, and love—the needs of the living
> creature, because it is a living creature (236).

What Sammler resists in Emerson is the predilection for a
priori arguments. "Consolers cannot always be truthful" (237).
What he resists in Melville is the impossibility of reconciliation. Man cannot know, since "existence was not accountable
to him" (277), but he must function; he must exercise his
powers as intermediate judge of his experience. Sammler must
avoid being locked into the paralysis of paradox. He must
"meet—through all the confusion and degraded clowning of
this life through which we are speeding . . . the terms of his
contract" (313).

Sammler, with his "one good eye" and the strongest sense of
personhood ("I") in any of Bellow's novels, incorporates the
strengths of both Emerson's belief in vision and Melville's belief
in invention, while still cautioning himself about their separate
consequences. One must be prepared to sacrifice reason when
one encounters reason-defying situations; one must be wary of
epiphanies that tend to console rather than inform; one must
guard against a stasis predicated on the belief that every condition of life stands in contradiction to every other condition.
In the creation of this protagonist, Bellow generates a new
American Adam transmogrified by his death and rebirth in
modern history, one ready to fly "outward from this planet"

with a clear sense of where he has been and where he is going, with one "good eye" firmly fixed on future horizons. Bellow's Adam knows that he must negotiate his present on the basis of his understanding of his past; that he must open himself to life's adventures without imposing on them a priori meanings or philosophical tautologies; and that he must celebrate life's values as they arise, "for that is the truth of it" (313).

Humboldt's Gift explores just what "life's values as they arise" may be, how they may become apparent. Charles Citrine comes to understand that receptivity and love bring order and meaning to life. Receptivity allows one to appreciate and value a thing when it is found; love occasions receptivity. The "gift" of the title refers not only to a hit film Humboldt leaves Charlie, saving him from financial ruin; it is also a human legacy of forgiveness for old disputes and past indifference. As Humboldt conveys in his last letter to Charlie, "Be sure that if there is a hereafter I will be pulling for you." [13]

Less personal and more public than Citrine, Albert Corde takes on the moral issues of his time as one who has "come to give support." [14] He travels to his mother-in-law's deathbed in Bucharest with his wife and consciously tests his reserves as a good husband, clear thinker, responsible citizen. His private ruminations reflect his public postures: a series of articles in *Harper's* lambasting the corruption and moral decay of our cities; an investigation of the murder of one of his students in a Chicago university—"one of those choking, peak-of-summer, urban-nightmare, sexual and obscene, running-bare times, and death panting behind" (38). His assessments bear close parallels to Sammler's in what they attempt to speak to the whole of mankind, to remind us of what we once were and have since forgotten or stopped trying to regrasp.

Bellow's heroes have an additional spot on the horizon to contemplate, that of their rich cultural history, their Jewishness. Frequently their own marginal status seems an apt metaphor for the modern condition, for the often repeated role of the American cut off from his cultural past. Unlike a Huck Finn's hunger for experience, a Gatsby's innocence in the face of experience, or a Nick Adams's defense against the full impact of experience, Bellow's protagonists do not merely continue the tradition of American innocents initiated into experience; they modify it. As European Jews with a rich cultural history and an ancient past, their "I" is not so much in need of experience as it is in need of a way to give experience a cohesive form. For Bellow's heroes, identity is not in doubt; the question is how to express that identity, how to give it its greatest latitude and freedom as the true mediator between perception and action. Bellow's heroes continue to come to terms with the self not to satisfy a metaphysical desire to know or a religious desire to affirm, but to satisfy an ethical desire to act rightly.

Further, the Jewish consciousness of Bellow's heroes carries within it an affirmation stamped neither by religious orthodoxy nor by national experience. It draws from our ancient emphasis on the fundamental worth of life and the possibility of humanity. It gathers tenacity from the collective experience of a people who have withstood genocide to make a living emblem marked "survivor." It is a spirit perhaps best summarized by Bernard Malamud's convictions about the direction of modern life:

> My premise is that we will not destroy each other. My premise is that we will live on. We will seek a better life. We may not become better, but at least we will seek betterment.[15]

This drive to seek betterment continues to absorb Bellow's protagonists. It is the index to the health of their eyes, the horizon against which their discoveries are made and their dramas played out. Rooted in a history of personal sacrifice and cultural survival, Bellow's heroes cease to argue with despair.[16] Instead, they ask, "In what form shall life be justified?" In continuing to pose this question in a variety of situations and for a variety of men, Bellow's work projects a sense of the self and of human values which are not only Jewish but American, not only modern but historical. In dramatizing the question of conscience, Bellow asks some of the most complicated and earned questions about our heritage, about the complex fate of being American.

Chapter Two

Retreat and Reentry

*"A hibernation is a covert preparation for
a more overt action."*
  Ellison, *The Invisible Man*

"*T*he dream of man's heart, however much we may distrust and resent it, is that life may complete itself in significant pattern. Some incomprehensible way. Before death" (*Herzog*, 303). Expressing the motive behind humanity's dream, Herzog testifies to a problem of great magnitude for the American hero who believes in "the infinitude of the private man." The hope that life will assume a significant pattern through the "true self," will emerge to generate "true values," permeates and divides American fiction into two major camps.

If, as Emerson counseled, "most persons do not see things properly" and must withdraw from the welter of appearances to enjoy true insight, significant patterns appear to the solitary man engaged in meditative thought. If, on the other hand, as Hawthorne believed, the significant patterns emerge only after man has joined in the "magnetic chain of humanity," man is encouraged to find himself and his values in reciprocity with others. The result is a pattern of retreat and reentry which has marked American literature from its inception.[1] Since society—with its jumble of needs, roles, and conflicting interests—prevents man from discovering who he is, retreat is usually the first step toward the discovery of the self, as well as the significant pattern that supports and emanates from that self. Retreat is prerequisite to reentry; reentry is an expression of discoveries implicit in retreat. As Ralph Ellison remarks from

the invisible man's peepsight on human activity, "A hibernation is a covert preparation for a more overt action." The pattern
of retreat and reentry is, of course, an archetype much larger
and more encompassing than its American version; as Ortega
y Gasset has said, "Without a strategic retreat into the self,
without vigilant thought, human life is impossible." [2]

Yet the American experience, with its emphasis on an experiment in living, a city on the hill, a journey on the open road,
is the perfect paradigm for a literature of personal quest that
must find ways of reintegration into a sense of community.
Even the most cursory glance at a list of American classics yields
an impressive group of works whose heroes withdraw in an
attempt to discover order in or impose it on their experience:
Cooper's *Leatherstocking Tales*; Thoreau's *Walden*; Hawthorne's
Blithedale Romance and *The Marble Faun*; Melville's *Moby-Dick*,
Pierre, *The Confidence Man*, and "Bartleby"; Twain's *Huckleberry
Finn*; Hemingway's *The Sun Also Rises*, *A Farewell to Arms*, and
The Old Man and the Sea; Fitzgerald's *Great Gatsby* and *Tender Is
the Night*; Faulkner's *Light in August* and *Absalom, Absalom!*;
Ellison's *Invisible Man*; Dickey's *Deliverance*.

The impulses for retreat are both positive and negative; the
American hero who explores the possibilities of retreat does so
out of both a wish to escape the masks of society and a wish to
confront the true self. He withdraws to cease being bombarded
by impressions as well as to open himself to fresh sensations.
He retreats from the "machine" climate of the city, where man
is divorced from his inventions, to invite idyllic satisfactions
where man is the author of his discoveries. Retreat is both a
defense and an offense.

Reentry also arises from plural impulses: the need to escape
personalism or purely idiosyncratic experience, the hunger for
some sense of commonality with others, the simple recognition
that like Thoreau one has "other lives to live." As Leo Marx
demonstrates in *The Machine in the Garden*, the pastoral moment cannot be extended into a way of life, but it can provide
spiritual refreshment to strengthen the individual for renewed
encounters with society. And as Whitman emphasizes, individual quests are always personal *and* transpersonal; they satisfy

the intimate needs of man as well as binding him to a fellow-
ship he recognizes as "man en masse."

Through a series of highly charged mental and physical retreats and potential reentries possible only to those who retain
an openness to experience, Bellow's novels seek to discover a
"significant pattern" by which life may complete itself. The
problem is, as it has always been with retreat and reentry, that
only contact with the external world can prevent solipsism, but
too much engagement with the environment is liable to dimin-
ish autonomy and uniqueness. Either is a form of enslavement:
"The world is too much with us, or we are too much without
the world."[3]

Bellow's heroes walk this tightrope repeatedly, questing for
ways to preserve their private patterns of experience, as well as
ways to relate to history, the larger pattern of humanity's experience. Bellow's instinct has been to return for artistic and
ideological sustenance to Twain, Emerson, and Melville—to
the slippery heroism and colloquial rhythms of Huck, the rigorous obligations of "man thinking," the dark, surrealistic subjectivity of Pierre. His heroes are marginal men, "isolatoes"
who by circumstances of chance or will have separated themselves from family and friends and who must discover the significant pattern in their own experience before they can reenter
the community. Their quests are presumably for freedom, for
knowledge, for love. But true seekers, Bellow insists with
Whitman, never know where the quest will come to rest. Freedom, knowledge, and love are merely versions of the quest;
they give the quest its form without determining its end. What
Bellow's heroes recognize is that reality eludes and transcends
the versions one makes of it. What remains is the gift of awareness that man has received on the journey, as well as his willingness to continue.

While Bellow employs, then, an American archetypal pattern of retreat and reentry in his fiction, his heroes reverse the
schema devised by Melville or Twain to represent the stages of
the protagonist's withdrawal. Melville and Twain begin with
innocent heroes (*Typee* and *Life on the Mississippi*), progress to
initiates (*Moby-Dick* and *Huckleberry Finn*), and end with vic-

tims (*The Confidence Man* and *Letters to the Earth*). Bellow begins with victims (Joseph, Asa), progresses to initiates (Augie, Henderson), and moves toward knowledgeable heroes (Herzog, Sammler, Citrine, Corde). This movement is significant, in my view, for it bespeaks the ways in which America has finally, with all due respect to Van Wyck Brooks, "come of age." Melville and Twain registered the cost of the initiatory experience in their own lives and art. Their sequence of protagonists moves from airy adventurers to embittered, suicidal, trapped men, victims of their own crushing insight into history. Bellow's protagonists begin as the beneficiaries of history, as "burdened men," and struggle to free themselves from the bondage of victimhood. As the book titles suggest, they start with a condition (*Dangling Man, The Victim*), work to a sense of personhood (*The Adventures of Augie March, Henderson the Rain King, Herzog*), and finally point toward an integration of self and society (*Mr. Sammler's Planet, The Dean's December*). Their retreats, then, are attempts to escape the psychology of victimization; their reentries are posited on the belief that individuals can control their own experience, defining relationships to history, country, and family in creative and sustaining ways. The struggle is a difficult one, and costly. Frequently, it convulses Bellow's heroes with the effort of Herzog's "vigilant thought." At best, Bellow sees reentry as a willed possibility rather than a certainty. That Henderson will circumvent the old rage and return to Lily and medical school, that Herzog will leave Ludeyville, that Sammler can survive others' endeavors to reduce him to symbol are alternatives rendered as *possibilities* only. Nonetheless, Bellow's fiction clearly suggests that withdrawal is a strategy preparatory to action.

Perhaps the most willed "hibernation" in any of Bellow's novels appears in *Dangling Man* as Joseph deliberately withdraws from society, lops off almost all contact with family and friends, and records his observations on life in a notebook. As he observes of himself, "He is a person greatly concerned with keeping intact and free from encumbrance a sense of his own being, its importance" (27). He is interested in his own motives and in others'; and the questions he repeatedly poses for himself in internal monologues are "how should a good man live?" and "how is my life justified?" He has tried Marxism in his youth, later to discount it as ineffectual. He tries an extramarital affair with Kitty, but abandons it abruptly when he discovers that it prompts contradictory actions and confusing emotions: "I have no real appetite for guile; the strain of living in both camps was too much" (101).

Joseph's friends offer little in the way of support or direction. They practice various forms of cheerful resignation, each attempting to manage the others' responses before they themselves are managed. This one-upmanship manipulation becomes clear to Joseph at a party where he sees his best friend Abt reenact the familiar malaise. Abt wears his quiet desperation like wallpaper, and Joseph is "tired . . . of seeing him rise to it like a jaded but skillful boxer" (47). Further, Abt hypnotizes the wife of a friend, a woman he has always had designs on, and humiliates her by a series of managerial commands. This corruption shocks Joseph into the realization that "we did these things without grace or mystery, lacking the forms for them and, relying on drunkenness, assassinated the Gods in one another and shrieked in vengefulness and hurt" (46). Joseph then is able to see the emptiness that victimization breeds. He is, however, less astute in perceiving his own leanings in that direction. He cannot generate new forms of freedom, nor can he settle for the constrictions of status quo victimization. He can, as Hawthorne said of Melville, "neither believe nor be content in disbelief." The war looms in front of him as an attractive tie breaker, forcing his internal dialectic to a crisis. Yet the society that erupted in war and that stands to inherit the fruits of war is repugnant to him. He observes, "Of course, I hope to survive. But I would rather be a victim than a beneficiary" (84).

In the light of these recognitions, Joseph's alienation solidifies into a solitary life except for a few minor acquaintances and a Dostoevskian alter ego he names *Tu As Raison Aussi*, a second self with whom he quarrels, alone in his room. Caught between this alienation and the desire for cohesion with his fellowmen, he decides to break the deadlock by volunteering for the army.

If I had *Tu As Raison Aussi* with me today, I could tell him that the highest "ideal construction" is the one that unlocks the imprisoning self.
We struggle perpetually to free ourselves. Or, to put it somewhat differently, while we seem so intently and even desperately to be holding onto ourselves, we would far rather give ourselves away. We do not know how. So, at times, we throw ourselves away. When what we really want is to stop living so exclusively and vainly for our own sake, impure and unknowing, turning inward and self-fastened.
The quest, I am beginning to think, whether it be for money, for notoriety, reputation, increase of pride, whether it leads us to thievery, slaughter, sacrifice, the quest is one and the same. All the striving is for one end. I do not entirely understand this impulse. But it seems to me that its final end is the desire for pure freedom. We are all drawn toward the same craters of the spirit— to know what we are and what we are for, to know our purpose, to seek grace. And, if the quest is the same, the differences in our personal histories, which hitherto meant so much to us, become of minor importance (153–54).

Joseph moves to break the lock on the "imprisoning self," and the tone of the last day recorded in the journal, celebrating regimentation, is the deliberate mocking alternative to the crematorium of the mind—a vault Joseph now believes devoid of all positive impulses and constructive initiative. Joseph must act if he is to spring the prison of the self, yet the choices available to him are cruel jokes. Although he may be, as critic Keith Opdahl contends, a victim of society, Bellow has used Joseph's situation to catapult him into a deeper exploration of his perception of himself.[4] If we look carefully at the conclusion of *Dangling Man*, moreover, we do not find a novel ending in willingness to be life's victim, to lay one's life on the altar of war; on the contrary, Joseph chooses to reject self-victimization. The end of the novel strikes out in a new direction, based on firm rejection of what is perceived as self-defeating.

Unlike *Dangling Man*, *The Victim* is not a book solely about subjective brooding but pivots on a highly charged issue of social victimization, the anti-Semitism paranoia that nurtures the prejudice. The issue of historical victimization, Opdahl argues, is clearly the psychology of bigotry. Jung, then Sartre, according to Opdahl, explain in this way:

> The anti-Semite's projection of evil onto the Jews is his attempt to order the world by giving tangible shape to his fears. The Jew, for his part, facing senseless persecution or the "sufferance" of others, may have as many fears and as deep a need for order as the bigot; he too may be tempted to posit an absolute evil and locate it—perhaps in a second minority. Both persecutor and victim live in a Manichaean universe as victims of fear.[5]

If the plot existed only as a means of portraying this psychology, it still would be a brilliant, if somewhat narrow, tract. It extends beyond psychology, however, to explore spiritual dimensions. Moving from a treatment of specific social relations to more metaphysical questions, Asa is forced to confront the nature of evil within himself, the nature of obligations to his fellowman, the individual's inability to remain an "isolatoe." The focus of the novel, then, is not on a victim-victimizer mirror reflecting Jewish-Gentile relations in New York, but on the levels of evil present in us all. The withdrawal of Asa illumines two levels of perception: the world of Asa's specific grievances, and the world of collective evil and fear to which those grievances point.

Asa's private world is already vulnerable prior to Allbee's appearance. Mary, Asa's wife and general security blanket, is away visiting relatives. Asa has heard disgusting racial slurs from his employer. Further, he is asked to shoulder responsibility for his brother's family at their time of crisis when his emotional capital is low. Asa's sense of persecution, heightened by isolation, is consequently based as much on real fear as on his projected enemy and double, Allbee. Bellow explores both the personal psychology of victimization and the real threats in the world that are capable of crushing Asa; the two are intertwined. Asa's battle is to separate real threat from imaginary threat—indeed, to perceive how one is the function of the other, and to succeed in escaping the paralysis which may be contingent upon that recognition.

For example, when his nephew Mickey dies, Leventhal fears

Elena's blame to such an extent that at the funeral parlor he is
certain her looks at him convey a "bitter anger"; he wonders
"what would he do if then and there—imagining the worst—
she began to scream at him, accusing him?" (*Victim*, 181–82).
Finding this guilt intolerable, he affixes "blame" on Elena and
her Italian Catholic mother, who he is sure sees Mickey's death
as God's punishment for marrying a Jew. "She's full of hate," he
tells his brother, who replies, "I never heard anything so peculiar in all my life. . . . Well, you've sure turned into a sus-
picious character" (240). Asa is jolted by this realization and
becomes convinced that the "fault" may be within himself. His
is only a partial understanding, however, and he backs off from
its implications. "If he were wrong about Elena," he thinks,
"the mistake was a terrible and damaging one; the confusion
in himself out of which it had risen was even more terrible"
(240–41). He even reminds himself later that "the reason for a
mistake like that could not be neglected; it had to be dug out"
(265). But when he finds himself locked out of his apartment
and Allbee in bed with a strange woman, he reverts to his old
pattern of projection. "He hated me. He hated me enough to
cut my throat. He didn't do it because he was too much of a
coward. That's why he was pulling all those stunts instead"
(277). When Allbee returns in the night to attempt suicide,
Asa throws him out in fear and rage.

The conclusion of the novel is not simply a rejection of the
doppelgänger. Leventhal and Allbee accidentally meet several years
later at a public theater. Allbee explains the abortive suicide
attempt as one without malicious design, one without any consciousness of "another." "I wasn't thinking of hurting you. . . .
You weren't even in my mind." His explanation charts the
larger arena of conflict in the novel: "When you turn against
yourself, nobody else means anything to you either" (293).
Allbee has some perspective on his rise-fall-rise pattern; he can
at least distance himself sufficiently from his own fears to recognize some of them for what they are. Blind spots remain: he
insists that his present relationship with a faded actress has
nothing to do with the sanctity of his wife's memory; and when
he sees that Asa's wife is pregnant, he cannot resist the barb,

"Go forth and multiply." Asa, too, has changed. "His obstinately unrevealing expression had softened," and he feels more curiosity than malice upon seeing Allbee. The chance meeting and intermission exchange is unconvincing, however, and nothing has really been concluded. Leventhal and Allbee's conflict has not been one posited merely on projections of fear and illusions of evil. While Herzog recognizes symptoms of paranoia, he also identifies real enemies. In fact, Asa's world has not been one of only imagined slights: Mr. Beard is an insufferable bigot. Nor has he invented a sense of oppressiveness: the squalor of the palpably hot third-floor flat where Max's family lives contains a dying Mickey in a darkened back room.

Bellow insists in this novel not only on the necessity of confronting personal fears but also on the urgency of coming to grips with the sources of those fears. Questions crowd in on the coattails of this insistence. How do I perceive my obligations, and what are my obligations to humanity? What fears overwhelm my sense of order, and what forces work to destroy my sense of equity? If projection is a way of camouflaging evil within the self, how do I confront fear without denying it? If affixing blame is an utterly inadequate way of proceeding, is the only alternative to believe that senseless or incomprehensible forces arbitrarily determine who I am?

Bellow's need to move beyond American naturalism is the need to move beyond George Hurstwood's gas-filled hotel room. The worlds in which the characters of Dreiser and Bellow live are worlds of difficult, often harrowing circumstance. They are worlds where evil exists, not merely worlds that go awry in the absence of good. Survival is all that can be hoped for in a world of random chance where a man, by an accident of birth or circumstance, can be crushed or elevated. In what form is survival justified and at what cost: these are the questions Bellow poses. And Bellow's work reflects the tendency of naturalists like Crane and Dreiser to write moral allegory, even in the face of a deterministic universe. Any sensitive reading of *Maggie: A Girl of the Streets*, "The Blue Hotel," "The Monster," *Sister Carrie*, *Jennie Gerhardt*, *An American Tragedy* reveals the "yes but" clause in American naturalism, the social protest that seems not only to want to picture the world "as it really is" but to cry out for its reform. If, as Jackson Benson argues, Crane, Dreiser, and Hemingway are failed idealists, then the stream that diverges into romanticism and naturalism continues to share its single feeder source.

As Bellow says in his Library of Congress address, "I seem to have asked in my books, How can one resist the controls of this vast society without turning into a nihilist, avoiding the absurdity of empty rebellion? I have asked, Are there other, more good-natured forms of resistance and free-choice?" Augie sets out to explore these possible "good-natured forms of resistance and free-choice." His function seems to be to exhaust possibilities, to mine every suspected mother lode. Though an orphan of sorts, life's most willing recruit, he is not pressed by the visions of victimization that paralyze Joseph and terrify Asa. Instead, he becomes a willing initiate—indeed, a professional quester who hits the open road with a sense of exuberance about its promise.

Augie attracts many teachers. They mistake expansive open-endedness for pliability, and all are hurt and surprised when Augie announces, "To tell the truth, I'm good and tired of all these big personalities, destiny molders, and heavy-water brains, Machiavellis and wizard evildoers, big-wheels and imposers-upon" (*Augie March*, 524). Augie fails to realize that initiation remains a suspended plateau of possibility unless it is translated into action. His only action is to evade, to "slip through" entrapment. In distancing himself from all the "destiny molders," he also cancels efforts to join any given sense of community, even to the point of refusing any close relationship with his wife. At the end of the novel he is wandering through Europe alone, and as his Russian friend observes of him, he "couldn't be hurt enough by the fate of other people" (453).

It is hard work, to convince oneself *for* and *by* oneself that one matters. But Augie triumphs in learning to trust the rightness inside his own "skin":

> It takes a time like this for you to find out how sore your heart has been, and, moreover, all the while you thought you were going around idle terribly hard work was taking place. . . . It's internally done. It happens because you are powerless and unable

to get anywhere, to obtain justice and have requital, and therefore in yourself you labor, you wage and combat, settle scores,
remember insults, fight, reply, deny, blab, denounce, triumph,
outwit, overcome, vindicate, cry, persist, absolve, die and rise
again. All by yourself! Where is everybody? Inside your breast
and skin, the entire cast (523).

It is the supreme work of the initiate. But as Ellison emphasizes, it is only preparatory work. Augie sees this work as an
end in itself. It is a brave first step, one which cruelly strips
him of the consolations of "crisis" history (Joseph's security) or
the consolations of a loving wife (Asa's security), and makes
him confront man's essential aloneness. Bellow shows how the
self, stripped of these consolations, ingeniously devises new
methods of reinforcement. (Augie, the orphan who refuses to
be "adopted," dreams at the end of the novel of establishing a
home for homeless children.) In setting Augie in space rather
than in time, Bellow suggests that man continually seeks to
discover his "place"; when the recognition comes that the Pla-
tonic niches may not exist to house the essential self, he scrambles
wildly. It is the first step into terrible freedom. And yet Augie
does not know what to do with it; he stands poised on the
threshold of reentry, waiting.

Augie's ability to slide through, to evade locks and traps,
even to wait, is not shared by Tommy Wilhelm. He can't wait;
he is a man cornered, and reintegration is too important, too
immediate a need to allow him to spend any more energy charting man's freedom. When we see Wilhelm, he is already in his
middle forties, an established failure in both the public and
private world, a dabbler in "freedom" which has now congealed
into a repetitive pattern of error. He is both financially and
emotionally bankrupt. He desperately seeks support from his
father, his wife, and Tamkin, a half-false, half-brilliant "guru";
but in each instance he is met with coldness and indifference.
His father refuses to assume any "further obligations" for his
children—it is a "cross" he will not bear; Tommy's wife is
blinded to his need by her own bitterness over a failed marriage;
Tamkin, while brilliantly elucidating the key insight of the
novella, takes him for his last $700. Compelled all his life to

make errors and to suffer punishment, Tommy can find no past or future key to his existence. Tamkin's message hits dead center: "The real universe. That's the present moment. The past is no good to us. The future is full of anxiety. Only the present is real—the here-and-now. Seize the day" (*Seize the Day*, 66).

For Wilhelm this is a gigantic release, since it focuses human energy neither on memory of failure nor on anxiety about death, but on an intense awareness of the "now" which has the power to redeem past and future. For this quality of awareness self-knowledge is required; and Tamkin's theory of the two souls, the true and the pretender souls, stimulates Tommy's thinking. In discovering that most men labor under the restrictions of the pretender soul, Tommy ceases to see his failures as personal, as exclusively *his* errors of omission and commission. From this recognition it is only a short step to confronting death, not as the final personal degradation but as the visible symbol of human mortality. While Tommy runs the whole gamut of initiation whose stages Ihab Hassan identifies as humiliation, knowledge, love, and reconciliation, one is never convinced of his ability to make real connections, to see the practical consequences of his profound lessons. His petty ailments, his secret slovenliness, and his urge for humiliation look backward to the self-pitying harness of Joseph's and Asa's symptoms of victimhood, rather than forward to the expansiveness of Augie, the robustness of Henderson, and the genuine respect and love one feels for Herzog and Sammler.

Bellow has said elsewhere, "You must manage your freedom or drown in it."[6] While drowning is Wilhelm's constant preoccupation, managing freedom becomes the central problem of Bellow's most likable and comic initiate, Eugene Henderson. His story is one of expansive exploration; his large and robust wife, Lily, the monumental Queen Willatale, the magnificent King Dahfu, and the shining lion are all emblems for Henderson's own spaciousness. Africa itself, with its primitive cadences, its vast expanses, its urgencies, its rages, its droughts, its mysteries and uncharted regions, its unpredictable changes, mirrors Henderson's own physiognomy and interior. To traverse Africa is to search Henderson's terrain.

Henderson is Bellow's first American millionaire protagonist; he goes like an Ernest Hemingway parody to the Africa of the big game safari, the dominion of the magnum rifle, the penetration of the interior by four-wheel-drive Jeep. Although Henderson quickly discards this apparatus (except for four $1,000 bills taped to the inside of his pith helmet), he remains an American in Africa and insists on translating his insights into capitalistic terms of productivity, GNP, and jockism. But however much he is "representative," he remains a "loner"; a man who sings in despairing moments from Handel's *Messiah*, "He was despised and rejected, a man of sorrows and acquainted with grief"; a man who has consciously withdrawn first to the pig farm, then to the basement room, and finally to Africa. Each maneuver implies escape *and* confrontation, for Henderson is questing for ways to quell anxiety, to confront death, to cease acquisitive striving. His search is essentially that of a pilgrim. Released by his money and his strength from material necessities and physical threats, Henderson seeks knowledge, depth of spirit. His journey succeeds only insofar as he is able to piece together one fragment of experience with another, to see cohesion, to see—as Herzog is to say wistfully—"a significant pattern." Henderson learns that whether "truth comes in blows" or, as Augie believed, "in stillness," what is of primary importance is man's ability to relate one fragment to another— to see, as Eliot said, "the whole consort dancing together." This is achieved in the lion's den, where Dahfu teaches Henderson in the dark, wordless presence of the lion how to be still as well as active, sufficient as well as pliable. And with this knowledge, however comically undercut, Henderson returns home. The initiate comes to the end of the open road and finds himself. For this lumpish bear of a man, "hibernation" has been preparatory to a "more overt action."

Herzog has been in a prolonged state of hibernation when his story begins, and he is desperately striving for a way to translate that state of suspended, preparatory consciousness into an overt action that will bear witness to the patterns he sees— both those he laments and those he celebrates. While Henderson's ability to see coherence, to relate one fragment to another, transforms him from pariah to returning hero, Herzog's capacity to see patterns everywhere pushes him to the edge of madness. For Herzog's overstimulated consciousness, experience is kaleidoscopic, each pattern dissolving into the next, each contingent upon the other, each composed of bits of glass which may center in one configuration only to appear on the periphery of the succeeding one. For Henderson, the figure in the carpet was singular. For Herzog, reconciliation depends on the coexistence of plural "significant patterns": a grand synthesis is not only impossible; it is naive.

The narrative pattern of *Herzog* is one of retreat and implied reintegration. "The main maneuver used to preserve identity under pressure from the dread of engulfment is isolation," R. D. Laing suggests, and Herzog's singular perception brackets the book in the sentence that opens and closes it: "If I am out of my mind, it's all right with me." In the opening instance Herzog obviously means, "If I am deranged"; his obsessive self-examinations, paranoia, and disintegrating health attest to that possibility. In the closing instance Herzog is punning on the phrase "out of my mind," since by at first retreating into the self and ordering it, he emerges as one able to turn outward— "out of [his] mind." "To live in an inspired condition, to know truth, to be free, to love another, to consummate existence, to abide with death in a clarity of consciousness . . . is no longer a rarefied project" (165), he says. For Herzog the unexamined life is not worth living, but to agonize over the examined life is not to live it. Even though his soul has been seared by nihilism, Herzog categorically rejects nihilism (an echo of Joseph's very early rejection of "hardboildom"):

> I don't agree with Nietzsche that Jesus made the whole world sick, infected it with his slave morality. But Nietzsche himself had a Christian view of history, seeing the present moment always as some crisis, some fall from classical greatness, some corruption or evil to be saved from (54).

Herzog sees that his own life has responded to this *modus operandi* even while he thought he was combatting it. Like his intellectual contemporaries, Herzog has assumed that the world was in crisis and that desperate measures were needed to cope with it. He comes to see that this view leads to "cures" hinging on romantic ego projection; that is, "we have to recover from some poison, need saving, ransoming" (54). Nihilism is just the flip side of romantic personalism, and the whole coin must undergo a radical exchange.

This rate of exchange is embodied in nine episodes spaced within the narrative and linked together in complex fashion by flashbacks to the painful past and fragments of the urgent present. Herzog's story begins in New York with the memory of his recent divorce from Madeleine. In despair, he decides to visit friends on Martha's Vineyard; but finding their kindness oppressive, he sneaks away silently from their cottage. Back in New York he visits Ramona, his present mistress, for a sumptuous dinner. When they make love, he later rebukes himself for this "feminine game." Remembering his own father's rejection and feeling that "he must do something . . . practical and useful" (207), he arranges to meet his lawyer at the courthouse to arrange for full custody of his daughter June. There he witnesses a criminal court session fraught with Dostoevskian drama and the terror of self-discovery. He runs out, determined to purge himself from the guilt the courtroom has uncovered, and flies to Chicago convinced he can "kill with a clear conscience" (254). There, at his old boyhood home, he takes his father's pistol from his desk and goes to kill Madeleine. Like Mailer's Rojack, he has entertained fantasies of dragging her screaming and bloodied across the floor, and momentarily he really believes that "in spirit she was his murderess, and therefore he was turned loose, could shoot or choke without remorse" (255). But Herzog refuses this American Dream, since it would involve an enactment of the very ideas he has rejected intellectually (crisis situations "remedied" by subjective violence). Further, his scrutiny of the house does not turn up a torrid love scene on the marital bed, but rather a tender scene in which Gersbach (the "best friend" who deceived him with Madeleine) is bathing June:

> In the rushing water with floating toys his daughter's little body shone. His child! Madeleine had let her black hair grow

longer, and now it was tied up for the bath with a rubber band. He melted with tenderness for her. . . . It was Gersbach. He was going to bathe Herzog's daughter! Gersbach! . . . He spoke with authority, but affectionately and with grumbling smiles and occasionally with laughter he bathed her—soaped, rinsed, dipping water in her toy boats to rinse her back as she squealed and twisted. The man washed her tenderly. . . . Then Gersbach ordered her to stand, and she stooped slightly to allow him to wash her little cleft. Her father stared at this. A pang went through him, but it was quickly done. She sat again. Gersbach ran fresh water on her, cumbersomely rose and opened the bath towel (256–57).

The scene depicts a justness if not a justice in Gersbach's tender treatment of June, and this pulls the props from beneath Herzog's masochistic plan for revenge.[7] In one of the final scenes, this justness is underscored again at the police station, where Madeleine appears to claim June after Herzog has had a minor car accident on an outing with the child. Madeleine overdramatizes her case; and despite Herzog's bloody appearance and ancient pistol (sans permit), the police sergeant, with some insight into the situation, lets him go. "Her voice went up sharply, and as she spoke, Herzog saw the sergeant take a new look at her, as if he were beginning to make out her haughty peculiarities at last" (301). Madeleine is not to be feared in this last scene—she is to be pitied; and with the reduction of her threat, Herzog is able to see himself as something other than "one writing under this sharp elegant heel" (76).

With the recognition of instances of justness in "ordinary life," Herzog need not make extravagant claims for justice nor search for the "extra-ordinary life." He regains a kind of equipoise. This balance allows him to go to Massachusetts, keeps him out of the hospital his brother Will recommends, and allows him to view Ramona as something other than a threat to his future. He has not, in Hawthorne's words, opened "intercourse with the world," however. And whatever health Bellow implies in the final pages, it has yet to be tested in a less solitary context.

Mr. Sammler's Planet explores the "hero" living, observing, acting, in his full social context. Artur Sammler possesses extraordinary capacities to see patterns operating in past history and outlines of the future. His "isolation" has dramatically real sources: he is old, with only one eye left after Nazi torture; his wife was shot to death in the same Polish pit he escaped from; his daughter is mad; and his only real benefactor is dying. He is removed from his immediate surroundings by his intellect, his fastidiousness, his wisdom. However worthy his reasons, he is not permitted a rarefied world. He is bombarded with "invaders" from every corner. The black pickpocket, Dr. Lal, the university fiasco, the hospital visits all rudely impinge upon his life. He must exist in and of his environment or fall to the humiliation of impotent privacy—a charge hurled at him in more ignoble terms during the Columbia lecture. Although Sammler is another solitary thinker ("seven decades of internal consultation"), he recognizes from the outset that he will never be able to "put together the organic, inorganic, natural, bestial, human, and superhuman in a dependable arrangement, but . . . only idiosyncratically, a shaky scheme, mainly decorative or ingenious" (234). And with this recognition, Sammler's key insight emerges: that significant patterns hinge on the application of different kinds of knowledge. In his youth Sammler had admired H. G. Wells and his attempt to explain the world and the future intellectually. But now, as he approaches the end, he reads only Meister Eckhardt, the mystic. Under the apparatus of man's changing intellectual explanation, Sammler is convinced that "we know what is what." And it is in the presence of death, extinction, "summoned to the brink of the black," that this deep creative, intuitive knowledge is most likely to be felt. That presence is documented in the threat of the black pickpocket, the extinction of the planet, and the death of Gruner.

Sammler is not looking, then, for Henderson's salvation or Herzog's reconciliation; he is not, in fact, obsessed with any personal fate but rather with the "contract" that is negotiated at the time of a man's birth—his relationship to his fellowman. Considered collectively, Sammler's contract dictates the fate of our planet. Accordingly, as he bids good-bye to Gruner's corpse, he says to himself and any God who may be listening, "He did meet the terms of the contract. The terms which in his inmost heart, each man knows" (313).

In his Nobel Prize address, Bellow says that "a novel moves back and forth between the world of objects, of actions, of appearance, and that other world from which 'true impressions' come."[8] The struggle to cancel out the world's distractions engages Charlie Citrine, in *Humboldt's Gift*, as he strives to locate the "other world of true impressions." Charlie's retreat moves him away from the world of business and power. His fate, as well as that of his friend Humboldt, becomes a metaphor for the "artist in America." He tries to wake himself up by confronting that fate and breaking through the distractions. Very like Henderson, he learns to accept "the terms of his existence." Like Herzog, he stops denying death. Instead, he suggests that he receives "intimations" of immortal life. Like Sammler, who reads Meister Eckhart, Citrine reads the mystic Rudolf Steiner.

> Under the recent influence of Steiner, I seldom thought of death in the old horrendous way. I wasn't experiencing the suffocating grave or dreading an eternity of boredom, nowadays. Instead I often felt unusually light and swift-paced, as if I were on a weightless bycycle sprinting through the star world (*Humboldt*, 220–21).

In reconciling himself to Humboldt's death, his life in the spirit, Charlie begins to live.

Withdrawal in *The Dean's December* seems not so much escape as an effort to go beyond society, to reclaim history and reassert culture in the face of the barbarism that characterizes contemporary society. For Albert Corde, the solitude of his bedroom in Bucharest opens the way to the inner riot of memory. While there is not much that Corde can do—apart from being attentive to his wife's griefs, purchasing cartons of Kents to bribe officials who control access to his dying mother-in-law, and reading his turmoiled mail from Chicago—neither peach brandy nor bed after breakfast can anesthetize his thoughts. Clearly, he shares with Sammler a full measure of cerebral complication:

he reads, he thinks, he teaches. Barred from effective service in an Iron Curtain country, censored by his own university at home, he nonetheless continues to address himself to the whole of mankind: its plight, its responsibility. He reflects on the importance of human life in contemporary culture, admitting that current wisdom on the subject "amounted to very little."

While he admits wearily that "understanding was at bottom very tiresome," he also suggests that "anger was better. In passivity you only deteriorated." He absorbs the criticism of his childhood friend Dewey Spangler, now a star-spangled international journalist, who suggests that his fulminations in the *Harper's* articles fell on deaf ears.

> In *Harper's* you crossed and offended just about everybody. You might have gotten away with it if you had adopted the good old Mencken *Boobus Americanus* approach. Humor would have made a difference. But you lambasted them all. Really—you gave 'em hard cuts, straight across the muzzle (117–18).

Corde understands all too well that his efforts to criticize constructively have been read as cranky and elitist. Further, he is, like Sammler, fascinated by the idea of life beyond this planet and his wife's experimental work in astrophysics, and the temptation to think beyond human history intensifies at the end of the novel. After he travels with his wife to the Mount Palomar telescope and sees the galaxies, he observes, "If you came for a look at astral space it was appropriate that you should have a taste of the cold *out there*, its power to cancel everything merely human" (310). Yet however tempting "beyondness" is to Corde, it is finally the "merely human" he comes to endorse. Corde is drawn to two human saviors: Rufus Ridpath, who fights for civil rights at the Cook County Jail, and Toby Winthrop, a heroin addict and ex–hit man who runs a detoxification center in Chicago. They are examples of the kind of "moral initiative" that draws Corde back into the present fray. Further, he hopes that science can work for the betterment of humanity; he entertains seriously the theories of a geologist named Beech who contends that urban hoodlum behavior is traceable to long-term lead poisoning.

The other magnet is love. In an important scene where Valeria, his mother-in-law, is on her deathbed, Corde recognizes its flinty yet tender power as the source of the support system he and Minna, his wife, manage between them.

> Minna said, "Valeria had a high opinion of you, Albert." Her head was down; she clipped the seat belt into place. "She trusted you."
> "You think so?"
> "What you told her last of all was what she wanted most of all to hear."
> No more was said of this. Corde was moved. His wife, unskilled in human dealings, was offering him support from her own main source. What came through Minna's words was that she was alone in the world; and with him; she did have him, with all his troubling oddities; and he had her (308).

As Corde observes after seeing the Palomar dome open to the heavens, "Everything overhead was in equilibrium, kept in place by mutual tensions. What was it that *his* tensions kept in place?" (311). Bearing the burden of his own understanding, Corde descends from the dome to take up the embattled present once again.

All Bellow's questers employ the pattern of retreat and withdrawal intrinsic to American literature. To search out "true selves" and to generate "true values," they go into hiding or take to the open road. Their rites of passage, however, begin in victimhood, move through initiation, and culminate in vision beyond the claims of personal fate to destinies inclusive of the human community.

Unlike Thoreau, who performed a "one-man secession from the Union"; or Whitman, who sang a song of perfect freedom; or Faulkner's Thomas Sutpen, who came down from the mountain to create a dynasty, Bellow's heroes see themselves first as burdened by their histories. Inextricably tied to events, decisions, and ideas that have spawned their individual life-scripts, they retreat to discover ways to avoid the cage of historical determinism. Their initiations move from experience to awareness, from determinism to freedom, from confinement to possibility.

Bellow's heroes do not have to "drive life into a corner," as

Thoreau suggested, to study its meanness or its glory. Cornered themselves by their lives, they are not herders. Like the protagonists of Dreiser and Crane, they recognize themselves among the herded. In the process of straying from safe pastures, however, they find they must reject both the isolated serenity of Walden Pond and the invisible man's mask of facelessness. Their critical discoveries ask questions that defy easy answers: how to avoid acquiescence to determinism? how to sort out real possibilities from romantic heresies? how to live life as human beings who are cognizant of the past, fully alive to the present, and fearlessly receptive of the future? Bellow's heroes learn to humble themselves before experience, but they refuse categorically to be destroyed by it.

Chapter Three

Reality Instructors

"He is arrived on a new continent; a modern society offers itself to his contemplation, different from what he had hitherto seen. The difficulty consists in the manner of viewing so extensive a scene."

Crevecoeur, "What Is an American,"
Letters from an American Farmer

"American history," writes James Baldwin in *Notes of a Native Son*, is "the history of the total, and willing, alienation of entire peoples from their forebears. What is overwhelmingly clear . . . is that this history has created an entirely unprecedented people, with a unique and individual past."

The alienation of which Bellow speaks is more than sociological and ideological: it flows into depths where the certainties of identity and value are wrought; it generates for the American a tradition of seeking the self as an individual, a member of a family, a participant in a larger social collectivity. Hawthorne, Whittier, and James all lamented the dearth of a "usable past" in America—a set of traditions and codified values against which one might measure his experience and certify its significance. It is a critical commonplace to talk of the American orphan, the Ishmael, the Huck Finn, the Leatherstocking, the Redburn, the Nick Adams—bereft of family and friends, cut off from supportive traditions and familiar ties—set adrift in an unknown and often hostile world. Yet the virtues of orphanhood have been insufficiently stressed. That American heroes exist unsupported by codified values opens meaning up to continual reexamination; since American heroes lack traditionally defined norms, each is the sole verifier of his or her own experience. To define oneself "by oneself," as Bellow writes, is both an American privilege and a hardship, both a frightening and an exhilarating process, which requires grappling squarely with the present while keeping a grip on the transiency of immediate time.

It is a terrifying task to discover America alone, as Augie puts it. To authenticate experience for oneself, by oneself, is an evolving process with many stages of development. Grounded in the conviction that dogmatic instructors in reality must be shucked off, the task of discovery demands that intermediaries, be they ideas or people, be discarded. Each person is both priest and novitiate of his or her own experience.

To borrow a phrase from *Herzog*, previous "reality instructors" for American protagonists have emerged from three sources: (1) the natural world, (2) intimate and familial relationships that form the basis of a sense of obligation, and (3) the understanding of history and culture.

Thoreau's *Walden*, Emerson's *Nature*, Whitman's *Song of Myself*, and Dickinson's poetry find "sanctity which shames our religions, and reality which discredits our heroes," as Emerson put it, in the "moral sensibility" of nature. Hawthorne's Hester Prynne, Melville's Ishmael, and Twain's Huck Finn find their definition within the "magnetic chain of humanity." Henry Adams's persona, in the *Education* and *Mont-Saint-Michel and Chartres*, and James's Daisy Miller seek to interpret and thereby integrate the worlds in which they move as self-conscious participants in history. While these sources of instruction are never wholly satisfactory in producing "lessons of the Real," they serve to define what the hero belongs to, as well as what body of experience he or she rejects.

Saul Bellow's heroes are peculiarly at home within this heritage. As Jews they possess instinctive holds on marginal "status," on the sense of being different, on the death of rural dreams, and on the press of cities. Further, as members of a group with powerful family ties, rigid requirements of fatherhood and sonship, and ancient cultural roots, they stand poised precariously on the tightrope stretched between the need to reestablish, comprehend, and ultimately honor the claims of family and the need to acknowledge that modern man is rootless, cut off, and that all he can be sure of is the "data of his own experience." While they feel these dilemmas with peculiar urgency, they eschew the expatriation of a Nick, the westward escape route of a Huck or a Leatherstocking, the "fugitivism" of a Compson. Instead, they remain *inside* the heart of American experience as special representatives of that experience, and are challenged to order it or else succumb to chaos.

Leaving his father's house is a particularly wrenching task for any of Bellow's heroes. Departure becomes a primary obligation for each male protagonist. The process involves a search for the father who is absent, or estranged, or uncaring. Moving toward atonement or reconciliation requires a rejection of false instructors—women temptresses particularly. It ends in beholding in the face of the father not only sonship, but the potentiality of the hero to be himself a father: a giver, not a receiver; a source, not a supplicant.

The search for the father in Bellow's novels does not become simply "the need of the Jew in America to make clear his relationship to his country," as Leslie Fiedler has claimed, nor is it merely a continuation of the need of the American Renaissance writer to find roots, to generate a culture against which the hero can define himself. Bellow's heroes, who have an abundant culture, search instead for "integrity" in the original Latin sense of *integritas*, "the state of being whole, entire, undiminished." As Augie March insists, man can be "brought into focus" (455) and can live in the fullness of his own experience. Bellow's heroes yearn to achieve an inviolate and expansive consciousness—humanity's true gift to humanity.

Seize the Day contains Bellow's most explicit treatment of this search. The very atmosphere breathes alienation. "The fathers were no fathers and the sons no sons" (84), and money is the only medium of exchange among men. Communication is no longer possible under these circumstances. "Sons" like Wilhelm continue to behave like little boys searching for their fathers' approval, measuring themselves in capitalistic inches in order to ride the commercial roller coaster to success. "Fathers" like Dr. Adler selfishly clutch their own withered lives, offering advice rather than comfort. Olympian distance rather than intimacy measures relationships. Human rapport is brutally satirized in the Dickensian portrait of the retired chicken farmer, Rappaport, who sits day after day at the commodities exchange greedily waiting for a rise in rye or barley or lard. Wilhelm learns, however dimly, in the closing passages of the book, that his failure to achieve success in a commodities-exchange world is symptomatic of his opposition to these values, this inadequate avenue of exchange. His capacity to "seize the day" depends neither upon his aggressiveness nor upon his ability to excel in the expectation game. It depends upon his ability to see relationships, to view himself as kin to all other men and to act upon this perception.

It is Tamkin who articulates this view, a character who is both "right" and a fake, a resource and a charlatan, a false father. "You see," Tamkin tells Wilhelm, "I understand what it is when the lonely person begins to feel like an animal. When the night comes and he feels like howling from his window like a wolf" (*Seize the Day*, 98). Wilhelm agrees with "this one last truth" (98) but fails to see the phony package in which the truth is wrapped. Although skeptical of Tamkin's motives, he succumbs to the need for a surrogate father and clings childishly to the hope that he may yet be saved by efforts other than his own. In the capsule of Wilhelm's intense need for kinship and for the compassion of his father, the love of his wife, and the respect of his children, Bellow concentrates the message he will repeat in succeeding novels: an individual is obligated to redeem his or her own fate; he is the father of his own dignity. Wilhelm learns that reality instruction lies within consciousness, and that he can cease drowning in self-pity only when he ceases to view life as a malevolent conspiracy designed to foil him. It is a profound lesson rendered in stark terms and falling short of application into action. Nonetheless, it provides a clear diagram of Bellow's hero's search for the father as well as of the related capacity to reject "reality instructors" in favor of self-sufficiency.

Although Tamkin is the first clear-cut reality instructor, Joseph and Asa display crucial relationships with their fathers which hamper their self-regard and lead them to search for explanations beyond those they can generate for themselves. Their difficulty in relating to their fathers results in a confusion of values; a distrust of women (except the "safe," and for all purposes absent, wives they marry); and an inability or unwillingness to father their own children—in effect, an inability to exchange sonship for fatherhood.

The important emotional transactions are always between males:[1] Joseph and Abt, Joseph and his brother, Joseph and his alter ego, Asa and Schlossberg, Asa and his brother, Asa and his brother's sons, Asa and Allbee. Recent critics complain that this is evidence of Bellow's inability to create a complex woman character; further, Leslie Fiedler suggests that this is yet another symptom of American literature's preoccupation with an exclusively male world.

More recently, John Clayton has argued that

> Bellow's women . . . are tough bitches: Joan in "A Father-to-Be," Thea in *Augie March*, Mady in *Herzog*, Denise in *Humboldt's Gift* . . . these women are versions not of the mother but of the father image. Herzog plays "Grizelda" to Mady. He is "female," she "male." These women have financial as well as sexual power over the protagonist. Tommy, Herzog, Humboldt, acquiesce.[2]

While these charges contain germs of truth, Bellow's primary concern is with self-discovery. He writes about the world he inhabits—a traditionally patriarchal world in which father-son relationships are pivotal. Sons recognize themselves in the mirrors of their father's pain, striving, achievement. Fathers see the reflection of themselves, their hopes, their inadequacies in the faces of their sons. It is the image of the self repeated in the faces of the male heirs with which Bellow's heroes must come to terms. Symbolically and perhaps even literally, the story of Joseph and his brothers informs Bellow's fiction with jealousy and disappointment, sibling rivalry, exile, symbolic death, and eventual reconciliation.

The appropriately named Joseph of *Dangling Man* is "dangling" precisely because he is waiting for an authoritative command to order his experience and certify its validity. He is looking for the ideal father, the patriarch who will provide a moral code to which he can anchor his own commitments. His family relationships have failed utterly to supply guiding principles. His own father is ineffectual; his father-in-law carries on a deliberate masquerade with a shrew of a wife; his profiteering brother Amos only patronizes him; his friend Abt has become cold-blooded and calculating. Joseph spends much of his life as a bachelor and wants his wife Iva to be subject to his strengths and weaknesses when and as they occur. He seems unready or unwilling to become a father; children are never mentioned. In an incident at his brother's house, he fights violently with his niece Etta, who closely resembles him; she is a vain teenager who has as many tantrums as he does, and who violates the sanctity of his Haydn record session by insisting on playing her Cugat records. In a violent outburst he spanks her, later interpreting his behavior as a thrashing of the immaturity he finds detestable in himself.

Beating the objectification of oneself and recognizing the face of the self in one's "attacher" are made vividly explicit in Asa's relationship to Allbee. Asa also suffers from a selfish and brutal father. "His father, who had owned a small drygoods store, was a turbulent man, harsh and selfish toward his sons" (*Victim*, 13). Their mother died in an insane asylum when Leventhal was eight and his brother six. At the time of her disappearance from the house, the elder Leventhal had answered their questions about her with an embittered "gone away," suggestive of desertion. "They were nearly full grown before they learned what had happened to her" (13). Asa, after graduating from high school, had become the ward of Harkavy, a friend of an uncle, and had been encouraged to feel he never distinguished himself in anything, getting his jobs through a succession of favors from distant friends and their associates. His relationship with his wife he considers his single stroke of good fortune, though he thinks she is an unhealthy cross between mother and madonna, seeing to his every need, providing him with the emotional security he otherwise sadly lacks. Other women are perceived, if at all, as either insubstantial

(Mrs. Harkavy), perverse (Allbee's whore), or directly threatening (his brother's wife Elena and her Italian mother). Asa's major confrontations, building to the climactic one with Allbee, are with males. Harkavy, who counsels him to grow up, instructs him:

> If you don't mind, Asa, there's one thing I have to point out that you haven't learned. We're not children. We're men of the world. It's almost a sin to be so innocent. Get next to yourself, boy, will you? You want the whole world to like you. There're bound to be some people who don't think well of you (88).

And Max insists that responsibility must exist distinct from Asa's "guilt." With Schlossberg, the Jewish patriarch who suggests that life is composed of choices and "no man knows enough" to reject "dignity," Asa also feels a certain rapport, which he manages eventually to understand at levels deeper than intellect.

With his nephew Philip, Asa feels a striking kinship that parallels Joseph's encounter with Etta. Asa recognizes, as he acts out the role of the surrogate father, how much he needs to rethink his relationship to his own father: his "payments," partial recognition of a debt owed, are not yet final.

> "After all, you married and had children and there was a chain of consequences. It was impossible to tell, in starting out, what was going to happen. And it was unfair, perhaps, to have to account at forty for what was done at twenty. But unless one was more than human or less than human, as Mr. Schlossberg put it, the payments had to be met" (154).

In all these instructive encounters, Asa comes to the conclusion that the "truth must be something we understand at once, without an introduction or explanation, but so common and familiar that we don't always realize it's around us" (170). The truth is as close as the Narcissus image: Asa sees his face in Allbee's, his own cries of victimization in Allbee and Elena, his own evasions of responsibility in Max, and his yearning for sonship in Philip. In the reflection of these experiences, Asa sees, however murkily, his own image. In recognizing this image, he makes peace with his heritage and, as the novel ends, begins a lineage of his own.

Augie's and Henderson's encounters with reality instructors hinge less on their relationships with their own physical fathers than on self-imposed blueprints of instruction. Both view life as a cornucopia of lessons spilling out in endless array for the eager novitiate. Both stress the importance of mobility, of independence, of continual reinstruction. If Joseph and Asa are capable finally of discerning their reflections in the pool of their collective experience, Augie and Henderson hit the road to multiply those reflections. Each searches for the ultimate verifier of his experience. Augie believes truth will emerge in the axial lines perceived in stillness. Henderson believes in the certainty of justice, its impact felt in blows. Each rejects a series of teachers' "versions of the real," yet each continues to believe in an ideal version, a harmonious way of living in concert with one's fellowman while still pursuing an "independent fate."[3] This belief transforms Augie into a perpetual boy, an aging Peter Pan wandering about Europe alone, unable to right his experience but even less able to admit that it cannot, in its present terms, be righted. He continues to reject mythmakers and "destiny molders" (*Augie March*, 524), yet he courts the belief that the axial lines will emerge to fire his imagination with hope. Henderson, unlike Augie, can return from exile to a New-found-land, reborn in the knowledge of the lion, schooled in the lessons of Dahfu and Queen Willatale. The land is barren, however. Henderson has found energy and joy, but he celebrates it on an unpeopled, icebound wasteland. On his way, he is not yet home.

Moses Herzog is. He puts reality instruction to its severest tests, asks of it the most complicated questions, and arrives at the most complex conclusions. Like Augie and Henderson, Herzog has been a romantic quester—a knight in search of the grand synthesis. Like Joseph's and Asa's, Herzog's need for self-authentication hinges on personal complications with his father. His legacy of doubt and guilt has been transferred, in turn, to his failed marriages. Herzog's "lessons" encompass the ideological configurations that literature, history, and philosophy have generated to explain human experience, as well as his personal, firsthand involvements with contradictory notions of equity, justice, and fidelity. His battleground is precisely at the nexus of historical justification and personal rationalization. He finds both wanting.

His looking glass is the wreckage of his life. He has abandoned teaching to reexamine the whole philosophical stance he once thought safely "synthesized." His first wife, Daisy, has custody of his son Marco, and his second wife, Madeleine, of his daughter June. His brothers don't understand him, and his closest friend, Valentine Gersbach, has become Madeleine's lover. His only real relationship is an affair with the forty-year-old Ramona, whom he can't help satirizing as a "priestess of Isis." He is, in short, required to rethink all his original premises, to meet life head on without the intermediary interpretations of "ideal constructions." In searching for a viable world view, Herzog collects, shuffles, and reorganizes the problems presented in Bellow's previous novels: the acceptance of human finitude, the incomprehensible complexity of truth, the need to believe in reason, the significance of choice in determining the direction and quality of one's life.

Herzog wishes to believe, as do all Bellow's heroes, that life has transcendent meaning. Yet the current systematic views of man, the "canned goods of the intellectuals," offend his sense of individual complexity and worth. Life is too complicated, too real, too mysterious to be reduced to a formula. He writes:

We are talking about the whole life of mankind. The subject is too great, too deep for such weakness, cowardice. . . . A merely aesthetic critique of modern history! After the wars and mass killings! . . . As the dead go their way, you want to call to them, but they depart in a black cloud of faces, souls. They flow out in smoke from the extermination chimneys, and leave you in the clear light of historical success—the technical success of the West. Then you know with a crash of the blood that mankind is making it—making it in glory though deafened by the explosions of blood. Unified by the horrible wars, instructed in our brutal stupidity by revolutions, by engineered famines directed by "ideologists" (75).

Even this "crisis instruction" known "in the blood" is too far removed from "ordinary experience" to suit Herzog. "No philosopher knows what the ordinary is, has not fallen into it deeply enough. . . . The strength of a man's virtue or spiritual capacity [is] measured by his ordinary life" (106). All systems spun by theorists caught in crisis history Herzog calls "reality instructors. They want to teach you—to punish you with—the lessons of the Real" (125). This view of life, which stresses the high value of suffering, "was becoming the up-to-date and almost conventional way of looking at any single life" (93). Herzog's whole struggle is to free himself from this view. While he recognizes that he is still a "slave to Papa's pain" (149), he believes that suffering is not the seat of wisdom, that "more commonly suffering breaks people, crushes them, and is simply unilluminating" (317). Instead of hugging one's pain in the manner of a Tommy Wilhelm, Herzog believes that one must be forgiving, affirmative, even magnanimous. He attempts this in coming to peace with his father's memory on the abortive trip to Chicago, with Madeleine and Valentine, and even with little June: "Coming to offset the influence of Gersbach, and to give her the benefit of his own self—man and father, et cetera—what did he do but bang into a pole. . . . He seemed to have come to the end of *that*" (285). Most important, he forgives Ramona and even himself.

Humanity's struggle, as seen through the lens of Herzog's experience, does not have to be given a systematic meaning: it is richer, more complex than any meaning man could assign to it. Reality instructors try to assign such a meaning because they fear endorsing "ordinary life"; they hope for official sanction because they fear living in the here and now. Their inflated models of life are caricatures of the real thing[4] because "the soul lives freely, expansively, in modalities we may not know. Three thousand million human beings exist, each with *some* possessions, each a microcosmos, each infinitely precious, each with a peculiar treasure. There is a distant garden where curious objects grow, and there, in a lovely dusk of green, the heart of Moses E. Herzog hangs like a peach" (175). Herzog discovers his own peculiar treasure by coming to terms with himself

through his memory of his father, his divorces, and the courtroom drama at the end of the book.

In his trip to Chicago to avenge the Gersbach affair, Herzog
visits his late father's house where his "very ancient stepmother"
lives, "quite alone in this small museum of the Herzogs" (243).
In talking with the old woman, sitting amidst the painfully
familiar photographs, Herzog recalls the day a year before his
father's death when Papa threatened to shoot him. Moses had
come for a loan and to commiserate about his failing first marriage, arriving "as a prodigal son, admitting the worst and
asking the old man's mercy" (249). His self-pity enraged the
old man, who, in a burst of hidden strength, seized his pistol
from his desk and waved it wildly at Herzog. In remembering
the situation, Herzog concludes, "The old man in his near-
demented way was trying to act out the manhood you should
have had" (250). Though he takes his father's pistol from his
desk with vague promptings of revenge, he has in fact been
reconciled to his memories, freed of his guilt. He recognizes
that no one knows the extent and degree of his effect on another.
"Who knows whether Moses shortened his [Papa's] life by the
grief he gave him. Perhaps the stimulus of anger lengthened
it" (250). Freed from fearing he might have hastened his father's death, Herzog is able to see himself more clearly.

The divorce revelation is another moment of suspended guilt
rendered in the shimmering flow of stream-of-consciousness:

> All this happened on a bright, keen fall day. He had been in
> the back yard putting in the storm windows. The first frost had
> already caught the tomatoes. The grass was dense and soft, with
> the peculiar beauty it gains when the cold days come and the
> gossamers lie on it in the morning; the dew is thick and lasting.
> The tomato vines had blackened and the red globes had burst.
>
> He had seen Madeleine at the back window upstairs, putting
> June down for her nap, and later he heard the bath being run.
> Now she was calling from the kitchen door. A gust from the lake
> made the framed glass tremble in Herzog's arms. He propped it
> carefully against the porch and took off his canvas gloves but
> not his beret, as though he sensed that he would immediately go
> on a trip.

. . . What he was about to suffer, he deserved; he had sinned sinned long and hard; he had earned it. This was it.

In the window on glass shelves there stood an ornamental collection of small glass bottles, Venetian and Swedish. They came with the house. The sun now caught them. They were pierced with the light. Herzog saw the waves, the threads of color, the spectral intersecting bars, and especially a great blot of flaming white on the center of the wall above Madeleine. She was saying, "We can't live together anymore" (8–9).

In this brilliant scene Bellow uncovers Herzog's masochism. His remembrance of things past is a Proustian world where pain both gives rise to and is projected into images of piercing light, burst tomatoes, quivering panes of glass, spectral bars of color. Like Proust's protagonist, Herzog is the victim not only of a guilt he feels he "deserves," but also of an intense consciousness that feels every ripple from memory's reservoir. Wanted or not, painful images push through conscious barriers to instruct reality in the torment of loss.

From this pictorial consciousness we are ultimately carried to the fleshy, odorous courtroom, where on the sweltering day of Herzog's self-judgment he watches a parade of wretched men brought "before the bar." In each instance Herzog sees a reflection of himself. For example, the young homosexual's history comes painfully close to displaying his own disgust with female sexuality. The child abusers enact a scene that Herzog has fantasied as his own a hundred times while "writhing under the sharp heel" Madeleine grinds "into his groin." When the medical examiner reports that the bruises on the child were heaviest "on the belly, and especially the region of the genitals, where the boy seemed to have been beaten with something capable of breaking the skin, perhaps a metal buckle or the heel of a woman's shoe," Herzog runs from the courtroom with the acrid taste of recognition in his mouth. No longer can he project guilt; he must come to terms with it himself. "I willfully misread my contract. I never was the principal, but only on loan to myself" (231).

Herzog has, by the end of the novel, sorted out the terms of his contract and reconciled himself to his father's disappointment, his ambivalence toward women, his agonizing love for his children. He has chosen to be, as Schlossberg would say, fully human.

> I am willing without further exercise in pain to open my heart. And this needs no doctrine or theology of suffering. We love apocalypses too much, and crisis ethics and florid extremism with its thrilling language. Excuse me, no. I've had all the monstrosity I want. We've reached an age in the history of mankind when we can ask about certain persons, "What is this Thing?" No more of that for me—no, no! I am simply a human being, more or less (317).

If Herzog's contract has been negotiated by the end of the novel, Sammler's is in evidence from the outset of his story. Sammler carries the notion of life's mystery to its furthest reaches. In more intellectual terms than Schlossberg perhaps intended, he explores Schlossberg's observation, "More than human, can you have any use for life? Less than human you don't either" (*Victim*, 133). The whole meaning of life derives from how we translate our own experience. The soul understands this truth intuitively, Sammler adds, for it "knows what it knows." No amount of intellection, no elaborate "Ideal Construction," no reality instruction can explain the terms of man's contract to himself.

> Being right was largely a matter of explanations. Intellectual man had become an explaining creature. Fathers to children, wives to husbands, lecturers to listeners, experts to laymen, colleagues to colleagues, doctors to patients, man to his own soul, explained. The roots of this, the causes of the other, the source of events, the history, the structure, the reasons why. For the most part, in one ear out the other. The soul wanted what it wanted. It had its own natural knowledge. It sat unhappily on superstructures of explanation, poor bird, not knowing which way to fly (*Sammler*, 3).

Yet Sammler himself is filled with explanations. He has been cast into the pit and has escaped. He fights others' tendencies to see him as a reality instructor, a reigning intellectual, a survivor of the Holocaust, a Moses leading the chosen from one promised planet to another, "one of those kindly European uncles with whom the Margottes of this world could have day-long high-level discussions" (20). While he, like Herzog, has had his "synthesis" (that is, Maynard Keynes, Lytton Strachey, and H. G. Wells), he resists formulas as rigorously as Herzog and sees beyond them with greater scope and behind them with greater wisdom. To Sammler, an "important consideration was that life should recover its plenitude" (19). This recovery is enacted when he chooses to "relax from rationality and calculation" and to allow the soul its knowledge. To further his spiritual evaluation, Sammler develops an abiding tolerance for all explanations: the lunacies of Shula-Slawa, the intimacies of Angela, the half-articulated consolations of Margotte, the academic pretensions of Feffer, the pathetic distortions of Wallace. In the cascade of words, the sad attempts at self-justification, the imploring gestures of self-analysis, he sees with "an intensification of vision" that man "does not know what he knows" (43). This recognition sets him apart, rendering him a commentator both on his own experience and on the planet's. Particularly after the Columbia debacle, Sammler

> feels somewhat separated from the rest of his species, if not in some fashion severed—severed not so much by age as by preoccupations too different and remote, disproportionate on the side of the spiritual, Platonic, Augustinian, thirteenth-century. As the traffic poured, the wind poured, and the sun, relatively bright for Manhattan—shining and pouring through openings in his substance, through his gaps. As if he had been cast by Henry Moore. With holes, lacunae (43).

Sammler is thus both distanced from the society he perceives and cast as an intermediary through which its perceptions pass. He is a cultural vehicle, in a way, bearing the testimony of this planet's experience at the very moment it extends its reach to another planet. He has been instructed in "lessons of the Real"; but rather than making of them prescriptions for the future or even, tempting as it is, explanations of the past, Sammler insists that "all are the terms of our inmost heart" (313).

Sammler's looking glass is the planet itself. He sees densely populated, teeming city streets, the looming specter of racial threat and sexual intimidation, the vacuity of "liberal" academic life, modern man's "peculiar longing for nonbeing" (235). But he also experiences Margotte's care, Angela's pathetic attempts at communication, Shula's crazy regard, and Gruner's dignity. In the one long speech to Dr. Lal, when Sammler is pressed to present "his view," he admits bewilderment in the face of the desire for nonbeing: "People want to visit all other states of being in a diffused state of consciousness, not wishing to be any given thing but instead to become comprehensive, entering and leaving at will. Why should they be human?" Sammler argues that individual worth cannot be denied, the soul cannot be declared dead simply by assertion. "Inability to explain is no ground for disbelief." Man "has something in him that deserves to go on. . . . The spirit feels cheated, outraged, defiled, corrupted, fragmented, injured. Still it knows that its growth is the real aim of existence. . . . Besides, mankind cannot be something else" (236).

Unlike Herzog, Sammler is not presiding over his own case history, an advocate at his own trial. "I am not life's examiner, or a connoisseur, and I have nothing to argue" (237). His is a distanced view, a one-eyed squint at "our human fate" as it stands on the brink of "colonizing outer space."

While Sammler's thoughts are centrifugal, spinning away and outward from the planet, his actions are centripetal, directing him closer and closer to the center of the city, the center of his relationship with Gruner, the center of his consciousness about humanity. He is no wanderer on the outside of experience, but a borer from within. During the frantic taxi ride across the city, a vain attempt to reach Gruner before his death, Sammler passes through the layers of "the real" that compose this planet's experience. The brutal confrontation between the black pickpocket and the Israeli soldier Eisen, swinging his bag of heavy metal religious medallions, the ineffectiveness of the academic Feffer, the impotence of Sammler's age, the transfixed crowd serve to intensify his real destination. "It was Elya who needed him. It was only Elya he wanted to see" (292). He arrives too late to be of comfort, but his words of benediction on Elya are words of benediction for himself and for the planet: "Remember, God, the soul of Elya Gruner, who, as willingly as possible and as well as he was able, and even to an intolerable point, and even in suffocation and even as death was coming was eager . . . to do what was required of him" (313). Man's ability to do, as willingly as possible and as well as he is able, "what is required of him" is Sammler's message to this planet, the reconciliation of man to his society, the ultimate legacy from father to son to father to son ad infinitum, the only reality instruction that counts. These are the requirements of leaving the father's house, enduring the pit, meeting the forces that conspire to reduce personal significance.

Clearly Bellow sees the risks. But he is unwilling to grab at the preprogrammed explanations of "nihilism" or "absurdity" simply because, as he has noted, "modern writers suppose that they *know*, as they conceive that physics *knows* or that history knows." Man is not knowable, life is not knowable in any such way. "Undeniably the human being is not what he commonly thought a century ago. The question nevertheless remains. He is something. What is he?"[5]

If Sammler, Bellow's deepest and most expansive intellectual, must learn to avoid reality instruction, Charles Citrine also worries about the intellectual's relationship to "ordinary life" in America. As Bruce Borrus contends, "Bellow's intellectual heroes are acutely aware of the reasons for their alienation from the rest of society, but they are unable to think their way through to an accommodation with it. Thinking leads only to more thinking—not to action."[6]

Humboldt's fate is Charlie's lesson in the failure of intellection, for he "had it all." He was "an avant-garde writer, the first of a new generation, he was handsome, fair, large, serious, witty, he was learned" (*Humboldt*, 1). "He had read many thousands of books. He said that history was a nightmare during which he was trying to get a good night's rest" (4). "Conrad Aiken praised him, T. S. Eliot took favorable notice of his poems, and even Yvor Winters had a good word to say for him" (11). But as Charlie learns, despite this meteoric rise to attention and power, "all his thinking, writing, feeling counted for nothing, all the raids behind the lines to bring back beauty had no effect except to wear him out" (5). Charlie must discover how to avoid Humboldt's fate by coming to value ordinary life, seeing the world as it really is.

Charlie also has a set of reality instructors who emerge from "Chigagoland." Embroiled in materialistic reality, they lure him from the snares of solitude. Rinaldo Cantabile throwing $50 bills off the steel girders of an unfinished skyscraper, Renata panting her way through an orgasm in the middle of the Palm Court of the Plaza, and the slick, modern, crowded restaurants of the "hog butcher of the world" are all tough and colorful "versions of the real." Both Cantabile and Humboldt are "fathers" to Charlie: the first schools him in the world of power and money; the latter represents the fate of the artist in America. Both are sources of guilt and confusion to Citrine, and both leave legacies that connect Charlie to salvation. Without Cantabile, Charlie would have an insufficient sense of the power of money, an insufficient materialistic drive. It might destroy him as surely as Tamkin argues it will destroy Tommy Wilhelm. Without Humboldt's "gift," Charlie would remain awash in guilt and paralyzed by a morbid fear of death. If Cantabile is the impetus to struggle successfully with the world of distraction, Humboldt is the spur Charlie needs to examine his guilt, confront his anxiety, and find in the world a spirit that transcends its boundaries.

Albert Corde encompasses both Sammler's sensitivity to human history and Citrine's dependence on human love to define the self. If Bucharest is cold and unrelenting, the United States is scarcely more rewarding. Underneath the veneer of respectable academic liberalism, Corde finds degradation and death. His brother-in-law swindles him out of part of his modest fortune, and his arrogant nephew joins a band of militants. When he returns to his home after the Christmas exile in Rumania, the first social event he attends is a lavish lakefront celebration for a wealthy couple's Great Dane.

Yet such symptoms of suffocation and decadence in both Communist and capitalist societies act as spurs to Corde. Perhaps he can prove, with Beech, that lead released into the atmosphere through centuries has been slowly poisoning the race. Perhaps his vitriolic articles on Chicago ghettos can help to alert people to the self-destruction he sees at work in American cities, if not entirely avert it. Certainly he has addressed this task at the conclusion, when he resigns his academic deanship and takes up his old job as a journalist.

> But for a fellow like me, the real temptation of abyssifying is to hope that the approach of the "last days" might be liberating, might compel us to reconsider deeply, earnestly. In these last days we have a right and even a duty to purge our understanding. . . . I personally think about virtue, about vice. I feel free to. Released, perhaps, by all the crashing. And in fact everybody has come under the spell of the "last days." Isn't that what the anarchy of Chicago means? Doesn't it have a philosophical character? (*Dean's December*, 278).

When Corde really examines the anger and hope that prompted his search for meaning, he discovers a need to assess cultural history and a need to honor human commitments. "What mood was this city? The experience, puzzle, torment of a lifetime demanded interpretation. At least he was beginning to understand why he had written those articles. Nobody much was affected by them, unless it was himself" (285). That self, out of love for his sister, struggles to win the confidence of her radical son. That self, immobilized by Iron Curtain regulations, tries to support the dying Valeria whose daughter he reveres. That self, mired in several failed marriages, tries to create all the domestic comforts of a home to free Minna for her scientific endeavors. As she mounts the scaffolding to Mount Palomar's dome, she becomes "Corde's representative among those bright things so thick and close" (312). He descends to the plane of human striving and activity to begin his task once again. While a "higher consciousness" is the goal, Corde's ruminations are intensely human. While self-sufficiency is rewarded, an "independent fate" is impossible.

Asa and Tommy find their "lessons in the Real" by examining the outside world and discovering who they are not. Henderson and Herzog engage in personal quests where codified instructions must be discarded in favor of self-discovery and nourishment. Sammler, Citrine, and Corde register the historical and cultural convulsions of this planet. Yet their greatest sources of definition and renewal are found in compassion and love for others. Each is an initiate into an experience larger than he anticipated, a "sort of Columbus" exploring a New World that he as yet only partially understands. Each struggles to answer the question, "What is an American?" The answers are as diverse as the protagonist's perceptions. But none doubts that humanity is worthy of definition. If momentarily defeated by circumstance or temporarily exiled by choice, individuals can return to reclaim ties to Planet Earth. Human destiny matters. And the working out of its meaning is the mandate of life.

Chapter Four

A Separate Peace

*"I did not care what it was all about. All
I wanted to know was how to live in it."*
Hemingway, *The Sun Also Rises*

"*E*rnest Hemingway was a fighter. He fought to discipline himself, he fought to bring meaning to language, and he fought to purge himself and his readers of the illusions, the sentiments, and the slogans of a genteel America."[1]

Perhaps because of the way in which he characteristically put himself on the firing line, Hemingway, his hero, and the code by which that hero lived served to define the values in several generations of modern American novels. Hemingway's heroes and their experiences were intense and insistent enough as models finally to invite challenge, even parody.

No more devastating or comic parody of the Hemingway code hero exists than that of the towering, sweating Eugene Henderson lecturing his native guide Romilayu on the "biggest problem of all" for the twentieth-century American hero: how to "encounter death" and derive from that encounter "the wisdom of life."[2]

> We've just got to do something about it. It just isn't me. Millions of Americans have gone forth since the war to redeem the present and discover the future. I can swear to you, Romilayu, there are guys exactly like me in India and in China and South America and all over the place. . . . I am a high-spirited kind of guy. And it's the destiny of my generation of Americans to go out in the world and try to find the wisdom of life. It just is. Why the hell do you think I'm out here, anyway? (*Henderson*, 276–77).

This "high spirited guy" stalks into the interior of Africa displaying selective characteristics of each of Hemingway's famous code heroes. Like Jake Barnes, Henderson views modern history as a wasteland, a chaos of conflicting motives and claims from which man must escape if he can. "Of course, in an age of madness, to expect to be untouched by madness is a form of madness. But the pursuit of sanity can be a form of madness, too" (25). Like Lieutenant Henry, Henderson confronts death and learns of love through an elaborate series of initiation rites conducted in baptismal mud and cleansing rain. Like Robert Jordan, he meets a fount of wisdom embodied in "much woman" and attempts to play the role of savior by setting, in an elaborate display of American ingenuity, a depth charge on the polluted cistern. (In what is even a more subtle pun on Jordan's bridge-demolition mission, Henderson breaks and then loses his "bridgework" altogether.) Like Francis Macomber, Henderson is the millionaire's son—come to Africa to search for lasting value, vivified in a confrontation with a lion. Like Santiago, who learns from the great fish what it is to live in concert with the natural world, Henderson is tutored by the lion under Dahfu's castle in the virtues of "Being."

In light of these parallels, there is little doubt that in *Henderson the Rain King* the parody is intentional and conscious; in his initials (E. H.), in his bulk, in his bravado, in the reminders of Purple Hearted actions, and in the ever-present pith helmet, Henderson is continually flying the colors of the code hero who goes forth as an initiate and comes to understand something untranslatable. The parallels climax in the hilarious, cruel scene in which Henderson, like a ponderous Papa Hemingway, dances the Rain Dance. He cries:

Yes, here he is, the mover of Mummah, the champion, the Sungo. Here comes Henderson of the U.S.A.—Captain Henderson, Purple Heart, veteran of North Africa, Sicily, Monte Cassino, etc., a giant shadow, a man of flesh and blood, a restless seeker, pitiful and rude, a stubborn old lush with broken bridgework, threatening death and suicide (199).

Obviously, Bellow is critical not only of the posture the code hero assumes, but of the attitudes behind the tough-boy stance and what those attitudes imply about the world and how to live in it. Bellow's heroes, from the outset, fight against the impulse to wall out the real world and live in the center of a self-created world built in repudiation of outside forces of destruction. Further, Bellow's heroes all attack the survival psychology of the code hero, seeing it as a set of purely defensive gestures leading to an orientation based on exclusion rather than inclusion, isolation rather than engagement. Bellow's heroes are interested less in acts that display grace under pressure (indeed they all lampoon that capacity with incredibly awkward blunders in crisis situations) than in knowing the motives, the reactions, the full range of emotional possibilities from which actions proceed. While Jake Barnes and his successors do "not care what it was all about," Bellow's heroes feel that "what it was all about" is their most compelling and crucial challenge, the whole subject and object of their existence.

Joseph announces at the outset of *Dangling Man* his aversion to "hardboildom":

> Do you have feelings? There are correct and incorrect ways of indicating them. Do you have an inner life? It is nobody's business but your own. Do you have emotions? Strangle them. To a degree, everyone obeys this code. And it does admit of a limited kind of candor, or closemouthed straightforwardness. But on the truest candor, it has an inhibitory effect. Most serious matters are closed to the hard-boiled. They are unpracticed in introspection, and therefore badly equipped to deal with opponents whom they cannot shoot like big game or outdo in daring (9).

He feels that the "commandments" of hardboildom blanket man's inner life and eventually stifle it. If man's inner promptings, his aspirations, his fears are not open to examination, Joseph believes man will live within a "limited kind of candor," which will support only a Me-versus-The-Adversary psychology. This psychology is precisely what Asa Leventhal and Tommy Wilhelm discover has marked their lives with frustration and fear. As they search for the "truest candor," they are forced to acknowledge a chain of projections that each has initiated to preserve his own view of himself as a victimized innocent. Each discovers that he has laid blame for personal failure at the doorstep of parents, friends, employers and has sequestered himself in a private world created for protection from other "adversaries." Augie and Henderson open the "serious matters [that] are closed to the hard-boiled" (*Dangling Man*, 9). Giants in feeling, world travelers of the interior life, resisters of others' versions of the real, they are Bellow's explorers who set out to discover inclusive rather than exclusive truths, truths that link human destinies rather than separate them. Carrying this search to deeper levels, Herzog, Sammler, Citrine, and Corde become the very best practitioners of introspection and uncover a dazzling variety of ways to "deal with opponents whom they cannot shoot like big game or outdo in daring" (*Dangling Man*, 9). Each repudiates the limits of the hunter instinct and the crisis psychology from which it derives. In its place each devises an equipoise, a balanced way of proceeding through life by living on the basis of one's own values while simultaneously tolerating a wide divergence from those values in others.

One might well inquire why Bellow set out upon a course of conscious and far-reaching satirization of Hemingway. One obvious answer is that in 1944, when Bellow emerged on the literary scene as a fledgling writer, Hemingway was the indisputable king. As Norman Mailer suggested, "Hemingway set the tone for us all, for an entire age." Monarchs attract as well as repel; and for a bright, young, intellectual Jew admittedly looking for access routes, for ways of relating to a half-alien culture, Hemingway was both an inspriation and a curiously limited model to observe. He portrayed with consummate richness and clarity the initiation of America's young midwestern sons into the blood bath of modern history. To come to terms with the blue-eyed WASP and warrior heritage of America in 1944 was to come to terms with Ernest Hemingway.

But there were other frustrations. Hemingway's adventurist fiction with its pervasive sense of risk no doubt seized Bellow's attention. The belief that man has only his own convictions to hold his life in balance and that "feeling was writing and writing was everything" seemed an attractive artistic credo to a keenly intellectual Jew whose every historical persuasion testified to the sacredness of the record. Grounded in notions of control, however, Hemingway's reverence for the word lay in "writing truly." With an unflaggingly clear and concentrated succession of words, Hemingway persisted until he "got it right." Precision of style guaranteed effect. For Bellow this one-on-one covenant seemed more tantalizing than certain.

To exercise control in an age of political chaos—of a second world war, a crumbling world order, and a desperate proliferation of explanations—was, for Bellow's generation of writers, only a consummation devoutly to be wished. World War II Jewish experience attested to little hope of controlling one's destiny, to the terror of the personal record, to the abrogation of all guarantees. World literature—with its mythic recorders like Kafka, Sartre, and Joyce—suggested that all stories are many-sided, ambiguous rather than bell-clear. Tip-of-the-iceberg assumptions did not always indicate the presence of a single, monolithic iceberg beneath the surface.

Narrative is less a triumph over experience for Bellow than a struggle to find adequate means of expressing muddled and often contradictory experience. While continuing to revere Hemingway's credo of the preservation of the moment, the sole importance of personal experience, writers of Bellow's generation found they could not reduce, exclude, limit, and still adequately describe the conflicting levels of modern experience. In Alfred Kazin's phrase, "History could no longer be reduced to style." Neither could history find its expression totally outside of private experience. Bellow found his challenge, artistically and perhaps even personally, in charting a course between the two: between the forces of history, which together compose that nightmare from which man attempts to awaken, and the sacredness—the inviolability—of personal experience as the individual lives it. In charting this course Bellow has come to terms with Hemingway's code and the guarantees of its nonnegotiable contract.

It is not simply the code hero as model tough guy or the exclusive requirements generated by the code to which Bellow's heroes react. They also challenge notions of instruction. Of pivotal concern in the code hero's hierarchy of values are the experiences derived from his initiation, experiences that quickly become lessons for the uninitiated. He becomes, in fact, the reality instructor. In the initiation process, Hemingway's heroes undergo a radical rebirth—a process that involves a sloughing-off of old identity, a complete transformation of beliefs, values. Their initiation takes place in a privately created, intensely insular world. In one supreme moment of clarity— spectacularly rendered in a mortar shell burst, a lion charge, a depth explosion on a bridge—the earth moves. Life is charged with meaning; man is reborn in the light of its impact. While the hero is reluctant to verbalize its value, his actions are symptomatic of the meaning and serve to instruct other novices who themselves will have to undergo survival training.

As is apparent from the internal explorations of Henderson, Herzog, Sammler, and Citrine, rebirth is not of primary importance to Bellow. Recovery is. Bellow's explorers are interested in sustaining who they are, rather than discarding that identity in the face of new discoveries; consequently, each seeks to reconstitute his identity by thoroughly understanding its motives, its needs, and its fears. The worlds in which they seek these discoveries are in Herzog's words "quotidian worlds"; they are not self-enclosed but lead back through wide-swinging gates into society. Hemingway's heroes act in order to survive. They assume an extraordinary history, a crisis situation. Bellow's heroes survive in order to act more meaningfully. They assume a quotidian history, a situation of common wants.

Perhaps the aspect of Hemingway's "version of the real" to which Bellow's novels register the greatest objection is the propensity of the author and his protagonist to become identical. Hemingway becomes the primary instructor, his hero merely the mouthpiece of his perceptions. One senses the extent to which Bellow defends against this possibility in the ironic undercutting of each of his successive protagonists. All Bellow's heroes are open to challenge. The reader is invited to find Joseph a stuffed shirt, Asa a habitual loser, Augie a cheat, Wilhelm a slob, Henderson a fool, Herzog an attractive compulsive, and Sammler a dusty, overly fastidious woman hater. None is without fault; indeed, it is as if Bellow insists that the reader find fault with the protagonist. He is not created as a spokesman for an inviolable truth. He merely "knows what he knows," with all the limitation and latitude that apply in each outlook. Bellow is quite clear on this matter. In a review of Philip Young's first book on Hemingway, Bellow cautioned against the dangers of authorial instruction:

> Hemingway has an intense desire to impose his version of the thing upon us, to create an image of manhood, to define the manner of baptism and communion. He works at this both as a writer and as a public figure. I find it quite natural that he should want to become an influence, an exemplary individual, and the reason why I think it is natural is that he is really so isolated, self-absorbed and effortful. When he dreams of a victory it is a total victory; one great battle, one great issue. Everyone wants to be the right man, and this is by no means a trivial desire. But Hemingway now appears to feel that he is winning, and his own personality, always an important dramatic element in his writing is, in *The Old Man and the Sea*, a kind of moral background. He tends to speak for Nature itself. Should nature and Hemingway become identical, one or the other will have won too total a victory.[3]

Critics of *The Dean's December* suggest that Bellow needs to be attentive to his own advice, that the reduction of aesthetic distance between the author and his protagonist, Corde, has left Bellow vulnerable to precisely the charge he hurled at Hemingway almost thirty years earlier.

Itemizing the chinks in Hemingway's rusty armor is a hackneyed critical exercise today. Carlos Baker, in telling us more about Papa than anyone cared to know, has detailed Hemingway's irritating propensity to preach through his heroes, his pathological jealousy of other writers, his dread of suicide, his pathetic antics as an aging soldier out of wars to fight. Even before the appearance of *A Life Portrait*, Hemingway had unfortunately parodied himself in *A Moveable Feast*, *Islands in the Stream*, and *Across the River and Into the Trees*. Yet it is quite a different concern to evaluate the Hemingway of the thirties and forties, to feel the full and vigorous impact of his work, which Bellow obviously admired when he remarked, "Clearly Hemingway, whether we like it or not, has found out some of the secret places of our pride and trouble."[4]

Those "secret places" figure importantly in Bellow's work. They suggest why Bellow's heroes show mind traces of code heroes even as they repudiate them. Both writers, after all, are concerned with ways in which man can authenticate his own experience; ways in which man can generate values within the chaos of modern society; ways in which man arrives at a separate peace, a contract whose terms he knows. Ultimately each writer comes to a different set of conclusions, but each describes the "secret places" that require the modern hero to come to terms with death and to escape the compulsions dictated by death psychology. Freedom, control, sanity are predicated on that escape.

The Hemingway hero generates an isolated, exclusive, elitist world built in criticism of and in competition with the "outside world." This created world affords the maximum of control, of safety, and of order. It provides a designated arena in which man can operate to evaluate his actions in a much clearer fashion—where he can, in Thoreau's terms, "drive life into a corner" in order to know it in its "meanness" or in its "sublimity." By virtue of its concentration, it provides an intensification of emotional experience. It is committed to, controlled and judged by, its own structure. Hence, it is the unique, albeit limited, embodiment of one way of seeing the world.

This perception is not without its dangerous aspects. It may give way to an irritating impulse toward self-assertion, for it creates a tendency in its characters to live at the dead center of this world until it turns overripe. The intensification of geographical isolation, the exclusion of other characters, the emotional insularity, close at their worst into a kind of prison and render the "created world" an increasingly remote outpost. The haven becomes the mausoleum. It seems, however, that Hemingway was willing to run this risk, since he devised the configuration in miniature in "Big Two-Hearted River" and developed it with fugal invention and economy in *The Sun Also Rises, A Farewell to Arms, For Whom the Bell Tolls, Across the River and into the Trees,* and *The Old Man and the Sea.* The impulse to create an insular world is one fueled by fear—fear of a swamping environment, of losing one's mental and emotional stability, of the constant threat of death itself. The created world, then, is a defense initiated to ensure identity, self-volition, and the ability to function.

In his major novels Hemingway demonstrates at least three positions in which the hero attempts to defend himself against a threatening environment. Interestingly, each of these positions is tested, then undercut, by one or several of Bellow's heroes.

The Hero as Exile

The hero comes to view himself as a victim of an empty and sterile society, a sufferer in a nightmare world. By believing in his own victimhood, he succeeds in separating himself from collective responsibility and guilt for society's crimes. Further, the posture of exile permits the hero to believe in his own moral superiority—he suffers for what he has had no part in creating. Jake Barnes and Lieutenant Henry stand at the summit of this position. Bellow's early works challenge this posture by requiring Joseph's reentry and by questioning, then denying, Asa and Tommy's claims to victimhood.

The Extraordinary Man

The hero constructs an identity to which ordinary laws and limitations do not apply. He is Dostoevsky's "exceptional man" and is defended against a loss of control by becoming a unique individual with a special destiny. His is an "independent fate." Certainly Colonel Cantwell in *Across the River and into the Trees* believes this of himself; and Santiago, in more palatable fashion, believes in his special destiny. Bellow's middle works test this notion and find it wanting. Augie is denied an "independent fate"; Henderson must cease grandiose gestures of "becoming"; Herzog must relinquish his desires to be a "marvelous Herzog."

The Hero in History

The hero turns reality into a rational construct in which he can live safely. He creates a cloak of abstract explanations to keep away palpable confusion.[5] He views himself as a "part of mankind" moving in the inexorable flow of history. This is certainly Robert Jordan's justification for blowing the bridge, his mental safety valve when threatened with impending death. Yet this very defense must be stripped from Herzog when he sacrifices his old syntheses, and from Sammler when he confronts the leering faces and catcalls in the Columbia lecture hall. In fact, Sammler, the representative of "an explaining age," very nearly succumbs to the historical imperative. Similarly, Charles Citrine, a Pulitzer Prize–winning biographer, worries about his "cannibalistic living off the dead." It would appear that Bellow's heroes to date find this defense the most convincing—so compelling that none of them is wholly extricated from its applicability. For example, Albert Corde never succeeds in forgetting that he is the "recorder of his age."

Each defense tactic is an outgrowth of its predecessor; the heroes who find victimization a workable defense are later supplanted by heroes who subscribe to an independent fate, only to be supplanted by those sustained by rational synthesis. Hemingway and Bellow, through the expanding consciousness of their heroes, ask tougher and tougher questions about the psychic life of the modern American hero. Their works reveal, in a series of progressive steps, the ways in which psychological defense mechanisms operate to sustain the illusion of control in a random universe.

Why does Bellow systematically reject the stratagems that Hemingway's code heroes devised to protect themselves from the chaos of modern life? It is tempting to suggest that Bellow simply demands better answers and that the age of the expatriate is over. While there is some truth in at least the latter half of that assertion, I think it is more likely that for Bellow's heroes—men of introspection, men continuously analyzing their own motives—these solutions are not adequate defenses. They are recognized by the psyche as false; consequently, they fail to protect against collective guilt or the terror of meaningless extinction. Hemingway's heroes succeed in valuing these solutions insofar as they bequeath control. They become the ritualized rules of a game whose frightening antitheses are sheer irrationality: war, suicide, madness. One becomes a professional. He substitutes rituals for the free play of thought, since thought may paralyze men momentarily in a world where agility is all that counts. In sharp contrast, thought for the Bellow hero is all there is. Actions are thoughts in motion; values, judgments, and decisions surface as the result of the continuous, often compulsive, examination of interior life. As I have noted in Chapter 2, Bellow's heroes move from initiation to innocence, from fixity to freedom, from game rules to improvisation. From Joseph's confident insistence that "I intend to talk about [my difficulties] . . . and if I had as many mouths as Siva has arms and kept them going all the time, I still could not do myself justice" (*Dangling Man*, 9), to Sammler's weary exasperation with "explanations, explanations" (*Sammler*, 3), Bellow's heroes live to explore their inner consciousness.

Even more fundamentally, Hemingway's solutions are movements out and away (even geographically) from the mainstream of life, from community, from any sense of corporate engagement. All his heroes' strategies point to the necessity for apartness. Bellow's heroes move within metropolitan life; their exiles and returns must be effected within the sprawl of cities and the conflicting claims of parents, children, friends, and spouses. All their strategies point toward discovering connections. These differences signal not only a changing portrait of the qualities associated with the American hero, but a changing emphasis in the composition and quality of "felt life" in the American novel. These are significant changes, ones that attest to Bellow's modification of a persistent tradition for the American hero, and they are worth examining in detail.

Perhaps the clearest paradigm of the "created world" initiated and sustained by a Hemingway hero is described in the account of Nick Adams's fishing trip to the Big Two-Hearted River. The trip is set apart first by Nick's climb to the high place, away from the low-lying plain. Some of the earliest details of the story describing the fording of a stream and the head-on confrontation with the cold, dry air of altitudes suggest a movement away from the bases of society. Nick's concentration upon making camp and fishing the river is recorded in a wealth of vivid sensory details. There is a ritualistic tone in the recorded act, in the creation of "a good place," as if the act were an end in itself and the integrity of that act were all that one could have. What has gone on before this expedition is never made explicit. Yet as Philip Young has pointed out, the staccato sentence structure, the half-uttered thoughts, the strict adherence to doing rather than thinking clearly echo Nick's present precariousness and suggest that the long shadows of the "other world" lurk just on the rim of his consciousness.

At first, nature seems to offer Nick merely solitude, a physical and mental place where he can make an envelope for hiding from a world "gone to smash." In that sense, the isolated world is a haven, associated with a high plateau, dry-cold invigorating weather, peace and quiet—a "clean well-lighted place" where man can superimpose order on his actions.

When this special place is juxtaposed with the wasteland imagery of the plain (burned-out land, blackened grasshoppers), it becomes clear that Nick is escaping the encroachments of at least two other worlds: the world of society as a whole, and the world of unbearable memory (of war, we decide later after reading the whole of *In Our Time*). The fishing trip to the high ground offers more than solitude; it is also a therapy. The "good place" is at two removes from the outer rim of societal obligations and responsibilities.

But Nick finds that escape is not possible, and that even in the security of the high country he must fish farther and farther downstream toward the blackened town, stopping only short of a dark and tangled swamp where fishing would be a "tragic adventure."

In succeeding novels Hemingway draws a continuing recapitulation of Nick's dilemma—that is, the avoidance of the swamp and the necessity of confronting it—for it also manifests itself in the night fears of Jake Barnes, in the ominous rain that soaks Lieutenant Henry and Catherine, in the need to function rather than think that characterizes the private world of Robert Jordan. Even the insularity of Santiago or Cantwell is as real as that of Jake or Nick. The hero has "dug himself in and is holding on grimly, but it is a one-man fight with no sign of reinforcements to extricate him from his position."[6] And as in "Big Two-Hearted River," in each novel the "created world" is set in relief by at least two other implied circles. First, there is always the suggestion of the outer rim of society where men are the possessors of a traditional code that the hero has abandoned. That Nick, Jake, Frederick Henry, Robert Jordan, even Colonel Cantwell once belonged to a traditionally oriented society is a necessary point from which to measure their departures.

The second circle, closer to the consciousness of the hero, contains his companions, his duties, his immediate surroundings. Since this world stands at one remove from both the outer rim of society and the inner circle of the "created world," it often serves as a double-edged foil, setting both worlds in stark relief. Also revolving on this plane, like little self-enclosed satellites, are the worlds of ritual: fishing, hiking in the high country, bullfighting. There are "interludes," "idylls," embryonic worlds that can be only temporary retreats but have such aesthetic purity that they serve as spiritual and psychological renewers. Finally, Hemingway constructs the world within two worlds, the inner consciousness of the hero and his "created world" on which he imposes order and meaning, erected and sustained solely through his precise control.

In sharp contrast to this neat geometrical arrangement of revolving but separate circles, or isolated and controlled levels of awareness, Bellow's novels describe a world that is all of a piece, incapable of being managed and controlled—a dense urban jungle jumbling all levels of awareness and action together. One level of consciousness spirals into the next; one set of emotions spills into another. The interruptions of a crude boarding-room neighbor invade Joseph's willed seclusion;

pressing family obligations, oppressive city heat, the continual appearance of friends and enemies play havoc with Asa's privacy; Tommy Wilhelm pleads for his father's recognition in a crowded hotel restaurant and registers his final failure in a commodities exchange; Herzog's and Sammler's retreats from the city and into "nature" consist of little more than short journeys to suburbia; Citrine is pressed and shaped by the speed and heat of teeming Chicago. In short, in Bellow's world one cannot effectively withdraw. It is a physical impossibility as well as a psychological and spiritual one. The world is too much with us, and as Joseph learns, "You cannot banish the world by decree" (137). Personal exile is as useless as postwar isolationism; one cannot wall out the world at will.

Bellow's heroes uniformly acknowledge this truth in their individual ways. They must divest themselves of claims to specialness; they must admit their interdependence with others; they must avoid the trap of moral superiority attached to the American missionary spirit. Joseph's enlistment, Tommy's heart's ultimate need, Henderson's lessons among the primitives, Herzog's recognition that he is a quotidian Herzog, Sammler's and Corde's rejection of the role of reality instructor all attest to the limits of the isolated, the self-serving levels of awareness that such a posture ultimately generates. Historically, geographically, and emotionally, insular worlds are useless to Bellow. They serve a useful function only as therapeutic islands prior to a reentry into a full sense of community.

This is perhaps most succinctly illustrated in one of Bellow's best-known short stories, "A Father-to-Be." Rogin, a research chemist of thirty-one, is on his way to visit his beautiful fiancée, Joan, who is a well-educated, loving woman with a flair for life and a tendency to buy expensive gifts. The story chronicles the events of several hours in Rogin's day, including a phone conversation with Joan, a trip to the delicatessen to pick up the items she has requested, a ride on the subway, and his arrival at Joan's apartment. While the physical action is spare, the psychic action is abundant; Rogin races through a series of temperamental highs and lows, and catalogs his chances for a successful marriage and his worries about his mother's future, his financial burdens, and his imprint upon the future. His mental turmoil is triggered by the presence of a fellow passenger on the subway who looks remarkably like Joan, who could, forty years hence, be a son of hers. "A son of hers?" he thinks. "Of such a son, he himself, Rogin, would be the father."[7] The thought terrifies him, since it represents the ultimate domination of the women he has both loved and feared (his mother, Joan). He suspects that his own child would not even resemble him, that the child would, with Rogin, form a category of "unconscious participation" in the hurtling history of life.

The recognition that man may not feel himself present in his own life, that son may not bear the imprint of father, that indeed "father and son had no sign to make to each other" leads Rogin into deep depression. The depression is one at first laced with self-pity, but ultimately it evolves into a peroration on the fate of modern humanity.

> What a vision of existence it gave him. Man's personal aims were nothing, illusion. The life force occupied each of us in turn in its progress towards its own fulfilment, trampling on our individual humanity, using us for its own ends like mere dinosaurs or bees, exploiting love heartlessly, making us engage in the social process, labour, struggle for money, and submit to the law of pressure, the universal law of layers, superimposition![8]

It is apparent that Rogin sees his fate as a common, albeit lamented, one that he shares with other men doomed to love a demanding woman and doomed to exist within the net of urban pressures and humanity's immediate needs. His resolve, upon reaching his subway stop, is to assert himself—to declare his "personal aims" and to avoid being "a damned instrument."

When he reaches Joan's apartment, however, his mood is radically altered. The Joan who greets him is a loving, attentive companion who brushes the snow from his head and shoulders with tender affection and offers to shampoo his hair before dinner. His troubled emotions begin to dissolve in the "hot, radiant water" and "cool, fragrant juice of the shampoo poured on his head."

"There's absolutely nothing wrong with you," she said, and pressed against him from behind, surrounding him, pouring the water gently over him until it seemed to him that the water came from within him, it was the warm fluid of his own secret loving spirit overflowing into the sink, green and foaming, and the words he had rehearsed he forgot, and his anger at his son-to-be disappeared altogether, and he sighed.[9]

It is significant that Rogin's frustration as well as his release is generated from within. There is no enemy "out there" against which he must marshal his energies. Neither Joan, nor his mother, nor the unsuspecting man on the subway qualifies. Rogin is his own adversary; he alone can effect his release. However, he can accomplish that release only through the acknowledgment of his relationship to others. He is repelled by the thought of being an instrument, a passive wayfarer in the "great carnival of transit," an image suggested to him in viewing the silent subway passengers. He longs to jump off, to exit at a station other than the one that leads him to Joan's door. But simultaneously, he needs to belong, to free his "own secret loving spirit" for others. His discoveries are mountaintop ones for him and yet are made within a full, even necessarily jumbled, social context. To comprehend his own secret places, Rogin must accept those who "surround him," those who—even while enmeshed in their own "personal aims"—help him to define himself.

Since Hemingway stopped short of that crucial step, Bellow's heroes also undercut the levels of consciousness that are carefully attached to the arrangement of space in the "created world." As was apparent in Nick's climb to high ground in "Big Two-Hearted River," the "good place" is a secluded haven that permits a perspective on the flatland below. Carlos Baker devotes a whole chapter in his *Hemingway: The Writer as Artist* to the "Mountain" and the "Plain," describing them as distinct realms in Hemingway's fiction. Despite E. M. Halliday's challenges, Baker's thesis that peace and quiet, love, dignity, health, happiness, and order are associated with the high ground is persuasive. The low-lying plains are associated with "rain and fog, with obscenity, indignity, disease, suffering, war and death, and irreligion."[10]

Besides the climb to high ground, passage into the realm of Hemingway's insular world involves crossing a body of water, an action which, itself, bequeaths certain associations. Jake crosses a mountain stream on his way to the Burguete high country; Frederick Henry rows across the lake to the Switzerland retreat; Jordan wades the river to measure the bridge before climbing back to the guerrilla outpost; Colonel Cantwell "crosses the river" many times on his last weekend; and Santiago crosses the largest stretch of water before staggering up the hill to his hut, the ragged masthead on his back. The body of water represents several things, depending upon its context in each novel: baptism into the stream of life, spiritual renewal, purgation, preparation for death, reintegration into the natural universe. Despite their variety of usages, then, the high ground and the river are distinct lines of demarcation for Hemingway, distinguishing both the exterior and interior contours of the "created world."

In addition to geographical distinctions (and their associated qualities), emotional dislocation and psychological separation mark Hemingway's "created world." The degree of emotional sensitivity in the hero is hard to measure specifically, for it is always conveyed by innuendo, by juxtaposition, by understatement. Yet the reader is always made aware that "not talking about it" is a kind of antidote for the depth of feeling. Unlike Nick's father—who can contend of the Indian woman's labor that "her screams are not important. I don't hear them because they are not important"[11]—the protagonist at the center of the "created world" is there partially because he *does* hear the screams and precisely because they *are* important to him. How then is the sensitive protagonist to fit in any integral way into the world in which he finds himself? Withdrawal is Hemingway's only answer.

In each Hemingway novel one can see the cost of this estrangement. Jake's physical and psychic wound will forever mark his separation from full participation in any of the other "worlds." Lieutenant Henry grows to realize that within his given world his "officering" is first rather superfluous, then ineffective, finally utterly meaningless. Unlike Rinaldi, he does not develop a special surgical skill that permits him unusual success in a wartime situation. Unlike even Catherine, who has in some ways become an angel of mercy for the wounded, a "cool English goddess," Lieutenant Henry achieves no significance; his ambulance trips are gray exercises in mud and confusion.

Robert Jordan's emotional dislocation pivots on the realization that he is "the outsider," even in his beloved Spain. A return to the University of Montana after his sojourn in Spain is no solution either, as he wryly considers a seminar on the Spanish Civil War—with Maria, among the undergraduates, documenting in personal accounts "how it was." Jordan belongs to neither world wholly, but rather has a foot in each—a posture suggesting not equipoise but a kind of desperate straddling. Indeed, he lies on the pine needles at the beginning and the end of his "created world" in as grave a posture as Cantwell assumes in the duck blind.

Cantwell's dislocation is all too apparent. He is a supersoldier living in a civilian world, a master tactician reduced to picking out an impregnable table in a restaurant. Further, he is dying of a case of pedagogical itch; he is running down just when he believes he has the greatest lessons to teach and the most receptive of audiences.

Finally, Santiago's dislocation is conveyed in his stated dilemma at the beginning of *The Old Man and the Sea*. Once he was *El Campeon* but now he "had gone eighty-four days without taking a fish. . . . the old man was now definitely and finally *salao*, which is the worst form of unlucky."[12] He has decided to risk everything and go "out too far." In a large sense, however, Santiago is not wholly cut off. By virtue of his recognition of the predatory nature of the universe *and* the predatory nature of man, he is in accord with the larger "world." His is a temporary dislocation, a battle to be fought within the arms of the natural world to which he belongs.

Beyond the geographical seclusion and the emotional dislocation, the "created world" is marked by a sense of sacrifice; it

is the effort made within this world that counts, not its ultimate success or failure. The reader knows that Jake's hell will
never be over, that Lieutenant Henry must "pay his dues," that
Jordan is so convinced of the sacrifice of his life at the bridge
that he is numb with surprise when death doesn't overtake him
there. Cantwell's story is a kind of coronary thrombosis in action, his erratic and laboring heart carved into his consciousness
at every turn in Venice. Santiago accepts a sacrifice of his life
interchangeably with that of the fish at the moment of the
strike. The characters within the "created world" are playing
for the highest stakes imaginable, with odds that are practically
impossible. Consequently, it is unusual if they move away from
the *faena* without blood on the stomach.

Concomitant with a sense of sacrifice is a sense of discipline.
This is caught best, perhaps, in Jake's rigid control and his
passion for the bullfight, in Jordan's intricate and precise strategy
for blowing the bridge, in Cantwell's painstakingly setting his
house in order (paying all debts, squaring all accounts), and in
Santiago's interior catalog of the correct techniques for beating
the fish.

But of what value are discipline, willed sacrifice, imposed
seclusion, aging instruction as the rules of a game in which the
"winner takes nothing" (except the satisfaction of his own su-
perb play), in the world which Bellow's heroes inhabit? While
Asa, Henderson, and Wilhelm could use a modicum of discipline, their problems hinge upon expansion of consciousness,
not reduction. They are urged to be extravagant, to "dissolve
themselves," "give themselves away" (Allbee's phrases), lest they
become fixated on their own reflections. While a degree of
spontaneous sacrifice has marked the careers of Asa, Herzog,
and Sammler, all are wary of the equation linking sacrifice to
insight. Each challenges the notion that through suffering comes
wisdom; love is more often illuminating than pain—the love
Sammler feels for Elya, or the sweet fullness Herzog experiences
as he paints the piano apple green for Junie. While seclusion is
practiced by all Bellow's heroes, Charles Citrine learns that
rentry into the community is of much more vital importance.
And while man's experience is certainly the arena in which he

learns, Bellow never approaches the Hemingway insistence that man must "be instructed," that instructors like Pilar and Santiago can assert universal truths not open to challenge. There are no heroes in that sense in Bellow's world; there are only men who try. There are no infallible teachers; there are only men who learn. The Game Plan is not understood, or its outcome a foregone conclusion. Life is too mysterious to know wholly, to schematize. The winner may take something.

The insight Bellow's heroes come to endorse repeatedly is that life is open, is possibilities, is freedom. The earth is "terra incognita" and, to paraphrase old Schlossberg, nobody knows enough about it for confident denial.[13] Perhaps this awareness implies, at least on one level, a new breed of writer poised on the brink of a changing relation between the American intellectual and the country he describes. Bellow underscores this possibility when, in joining with friends on the *Partisan Review*—Jewish intellectuals with strong European roots like Isaac Rosenfield, Delmore Schwartz, and Alfred Kazin among others—he contributes to the drafting of this editorial statement for a 1952 issue devoted to "Our Country and Our Culture":

> We have obviously come a long way from the earlier rejection of America as spiritually barren, from attacks of Mencken on the "booboisie," and the Marxist picture of America in the Thirties as a land of capitalist reaction. . . . Obviously this overwhelming change involves a new image of America. Politically, there is a recognition that the kind of democracy which exists in America has an intrinsic and positive value. . . . More and more writers have ceased to think of themselves as rebels and exiles. They now believe that their values, if they are to be realized at all, must be realized in America and in relation to the actuality of American life.[14]

Yet Bellow's war with Hemingway is fought on a deeper, more personal stratum than a discussion of changing attitudes among American literati would indicate. His allegiance to life is won only after his heroes systematically confront death and find it no more or less than part of a complex equation with life. The secret of Hemingway's inner world is, finally, that it will self-destruct. His heroes recognize this and acknowledge it with the bitter taste of self-deception in their mouths. Love and honor and courage are only temporary: destruction is permanent. Consequently, there is an abiding desperation about Hemingway's inner consciousness that bespeaks the sheer negativism of a failed idealist. As Frederick Henry asserts: "You died. You did not know what it was about. You never had time to learn. They threw you in and told you the rules and the first time they caught you off base they killed you." [15] It is a sort of personal testimony, escalated to universal comment, which generates "crisis history," the kind of writhing awareness that Herzog wryly observes "longs to be saved," the kind of consciousness that secretly believes in universal truths while simultaneously expending maximum energy in mocking them. While the failed idealist grimly catalogs death's inexorable victory, he half believes it can be averted, stayed, somehow outplayed, bargained with. All his efforts are harnessed to that end.

Bellow's heroes are quickly dispossessed of this conviction. In yielding up all vestiges of idealism, covert or overt, they are forced to confront death without the benefit of ritualistic apparatus designed to lessen its impact. If they are converts to reality, and if reality is finally beautiful, it is also—like Atti the Lioness—terrible. To confront one's own extinction is a terrifying task, particularly wrenching for a hero who prides himself on a unique self. Often it simply paralyzes Bellow's heroes. Yet it is the most crucial confrontation of all, and each of Bellow's heroes undergoes it.

Joseph can speak in bland abstractions about the casualties of the war; yet he is tortured by a scene he encounters late one rainy evening on a walk home when he sees a man fall down as if with a sudden stroke. "To many in the fascinated crowd the figure of the man on the ground must have been what it was to me—a prevision. Without warning, down" (*Dangling Man*, 116). It is only after Joseph acknowledges the reality of death that he succeeds in being present in his own life. Asa associates fears of death with the face of his mother's madness and must endure the death of Mickey before the straitjacket of his deferred guilt is finally loosened. From the aging inhabitants of the Hotel Gloriana, to images of hemorrhaging money, snatches of "Lycidas," and drowning imagery, Tommy Wilhelm's world is shot through with constant reminders of the possibility of his extinction at any time. Augie confronts death through a variety of representatives, none more convincing than the eagle Caligula, who, while "trained to kill," has other, more "human, redeeming tendencies." Through Augie, one sees the desperate desire of an individual to control his life, to preserve himself as a "simple, separate person." Death cancels out individuality, Augie learns, and he summarizes his understanding in this stark way: "Death is going to take the boundaries away from us, that we should no more be persons" (*Augie March*, 519). Henderson's first major test is the removal of the dead Sungo from his tent, an effort marked by futility and clearly signaling his own future fate should strength and energy fail him. His last lesson is the death of Dahfu, a perfect recapitulation of that reality. Herzog confronts both the fact of the death of his father when he returns to Chicago and the rehearsal of his own death in the half-formed notions of suicide he entertains when he sees his life on trial in the Chicago courtroom and in Madeleine's eyes. Sammler is the man who looks at death squarely, not out of an act of singular skill or monumental bravery but out of a combination of accident, instinct, luck, and the gratuitous compassion extended by others.

The confrontation with one's own extinction is an excruciating process, one which many heroes in Bellow's novels begin but few complete. As Allbee observes, "It takes a long time before you're ready to quit dodging. Meanwhile, the pain is horrible" (*Victim*, 227). It contributes in the largest measure to the central psychic crisis in the lives of Bellow's characters. Yet it is only after this enforced confrontation that Bellow's heroes can cease to expend energy in warding off the real and imagined threats implicit in death psychology. Charles Citrine, in the last scene of *Humboldt's Gift*, is at last burying his dead—the step he must take in order to enjoy life and live meaningfully. Albert Corde, whose "December" was a death watch, returns from the crematorium to view the stars. The coded rituals of "grace under pressure" cease to be important when one recognizes, as Joseph remarks in his journal: "We are all drawn toward the same craters of the spirit—to know what we are and what we are for, to know our purpose, to seek grace. And if the quest is the same, the differences in our personal histories, which hitherto meant so much to us, become of minor importance" (*Dangling Man*, 154).

With this freedom there emerges a whole new set of possibilities, a whole new battery of questions to fire at life. "There may be truths on the side of life," Bellow suggests in an interview. "There may be some truths which are, after all, our friends in the universe." [16] If, as Bellow believes, these possibilities are worth exploring, one is free to do so only after he is released from the anxiety of death's exclusive potency. Life's possibilities lie less in the marvelous playing out of a hopeless game than they do in the tentative, even blundering exploration of an as yet undetermined future. Joseph writes the real epitaph for the code hero when he recognizes that willed divorce from the world yields neither peace nor definition: "I had not done well alone. I doubted whether anyone could. To be pushed upon oneself entirely put the very facts of existence in doubt" (*Dangling Man*, 190).

Chapter Five

Technique as Discovery

"It is with fiction as with religion. It should present
another world, but one to which we feel the tie."
Melville, *The Confidence Man*

"No doubt the world is entirely an imaginary world,
but it is only once removed from the true world."
Singer, "Gimpel the Fool"
(Bellow's translation)

*L*ike many other fine American writers, Saul Bellow has essentially one story to tell—the story of a man dangling between two worlds, between the ideas, commitments, and value systems attached to each of those worlds. His hero is not a romantic rebel, but he has "opposition" in him; he refuses to accept secondhand versions of reality. Consequently, he becomes doubly dislocated: first, by circumstance; second, by choice. His major dilemma arises from his need, on the one hand, to maintain a sense of personal definition and his need, on the other hand, to affirm the values of the community. He is always struggling with the same question: what does it mean to be fully human? Bellow's answers to that question depend on his hero's way of seeing his world, himself, and his dilemma. They run the gamut of exploration from Augie's larky, boisterous excursions "into the real" to Herzog's brilliant mental forums of argumentation. The novels are all special forms of inquiry, asking questions in fictive form about one's purpose and destiny. They are not tracts presenting an argument for its own sake, nor do they exemplify any systematized thought predicated outside the novels' internal processes.[1]

Rather, emphasis and variety come from the ways in which Bellow has told the story, the windows through which protagonists peer. Since the lens through which we view experience accounts not only for what we see but for what we make of what we see, Bellow's ever-shifting artistic frames generate new ways of looking at his fable on modern man and arrive at differing conclusions about the options available to him. This chapter will examine not only what the novels mean but how they yield that meaning, how selected techniques are used for discovery. To accomplish this I will first train the telescope on the novels, looking down the corridor of Bellow's cumulative work to observe the changing faces of the hero, the variety of structural forms employed, and the artistic manipulation of time, weight, and space. Bellow chooses these artistic devices in order to reinforce his portraits of burdened men locked in time, in dilemmas of past as well as present, and the means by which each secures release and self-definition by determining his place in human history. The microscope will then replace the telescope for a study of specifics indigenous to Bellow's style and his particular brand of organic art, best exemplified to date in *Mr. Sammler's Planet*, though also accessible through *Humboldt's Gift* and *The Dean's December*. My argument concludes with a discussion of what I believe to be Bellow's greatest American emphasis through all of his changing narrative formulas, namely, the triumph of the imagination.

Bellow's narrative develops by unfolding the protagonist's awareness of the world and of himself in ways that suggest the imaginative power of Henry James. The germ of a James story is not a plot but the development of a protagonist, often one who is both overwhelmed by external adversity and at the same time ennobled by it. Like Winterbourne and Ralph Touchett, Charles Corde is "a moralist of seeing." Bellow has also separated the "exploiters" from the "appreciators." The former are persons who consistently use others for their own purposes: Tamkin, Einhorn, Dewey Spangler. The latter appreciate other people for their own worth, and so expand their own realization of life's possibilities at the same time: Valeria's family and their circle, who struggle to maintain a warmth, a human "connectedness," even in a tyrannical context. The unfolding of the hero's sensibility, one on which "nothing is lost," is both the experience the novel describes and the perspective on that experience.

Bellow creates a hero almost always out of synch with the fashionable posture of the times. Joseph's introspective dangling is posed against the collective, unified war effort of America in 1944. Asa is the 1947 Jew forced to give up his claims to victimhood. Augie is the resister, the adventurer who has "opposition in him," who, while he grows up in the radical thirties, seeks his destiny on the brink of the placid fifties (1949). Tommy Wilhelm feels his urgent slide into failure in the "I Like Ike" years of stasis, the era of self-congratulatory novels and films about the "second chance" success story. Sammler, the aged Polish Jew whose intellect was shaped by the Bloomsbury group, charts his discoveries in 1970 among members of the "Pepsi Generation." Charles Citrine is an intellectual, most admiring the radical leftists of the thirties, who wins prizes for conservative biographies. Albert Corde makes his observations on the death of our cities in Reagan's "year of economic recovery."

One can admire these creations simply as novelistic acts of courage. But more important, they suggest ways in which Bellow is approaching his material, both from within a frame at some distance from the ideas and values currently holding sway in the culture (like James's use of European mores) and from within a frame that is the product of that culture. For each of Bellow's heroes is the sum of current social experience as much as he is outside of it. Perhaps Henderson, the world traveler shouting in 1959, "I want, I want," and Herzog, the world-weary academician of 1964, most poignantly display the signature of their culture while working all the while, through comic complaint, to undercut it.

Why is Saul Bellow so consistently interested in working through the marginal point of view—the frame that revolves like a satellite around the culture to which it is bound and which it reflects, but with which it will never wholly unite? Beyond the arguments about minority status and modern urban dislocation, Bellow's is a conscious artistic choice, one which allows for a full inquiry into the nature of man's freedom and the forces that serve to bind and limit his choices. By separating individual man from man en masse, Bellow is able to comment on the constituents of each without sacrificing their essential relationship. No one hero belongs wholly to the culture he exists within; yet he is a composite of the charcteristics of that culture as well as a seismograph registering, by his very opposition, the ingredients of which that culture is composed. This point of view orders experience, creates scale, confers values by bequeathing first to the hero, but ultimately to the reader, perspective.

Since Bellow's fiction is a fiction of ideas, his characters are all advocates, carrying on in a constant forum of debate and action arguments over commitments, values, and historical justifications of one kind or another. But since Bellow so distrusts the "didactic purpose," his fiction stops short of demands for answers. His conclusions suggest James's dictum in *The Art of Fiction*: "If you must indulge in conclusions, let them have the taste of wide knowledge."

Bellow has caught his heroes in the act of discovery; his fiction is the recapitulation of that act. This is accomplished by an artistic centering in the hero's consciousness. He is the forum, his mind the internal debate. Within his consciousness all cases are tried, all positions weighed and challenged. All other characters exist as foils. Some are cast as false or therapeutic reality instructors: Allbee, Schlossberg, Tamkin, Renling, Einhorn, Dahfu. Others are cast as tempters: Sono, Augie's brother, Simon, the student activist Feffer. Atti the lion, Caligula the eagle, Smolak the bear are employed as miracles of natural persuasion. Within this welter of conflicting opinion, evidence, and influence, the hero moves toward his choices— perhaps none fully formulated or consistently correct, but generated amidst the strongest possible arguments pro and con. The strength of any given position is evaluated in part by the strength of its opposition.

In a 1962 essay, Bellow certifies his admiration for the "kind of didactic novelist" Dostoevsky was in contrast to D. H. Lawrence. He cites the letter Dostoevsky wrote to one of his friends just after he had completed the section of the *Brothers Karamazov* where Ivan argues with Alyosha against any possibility of justice. Dostoevsky mentions that the task now remains to him to construct a defense through Father Zossima, yet he has all but devastated his own position. Bellow concludes:

> This, I think, is the greatest achievement possible in a novel of ideas. It becomes art when the views most opposite to the author's own are allowed to exist in full strength. Without this a novel of ideas is mere self-indulgence, and didacticism is simply axe-grinding. The opposites must be free to range themselves against each other, and they must be passionately expressed on both sides.[2]

It is this invitation to opposition that most characterizes the Bellow hero, for it takes the measure of his relationship to his culture and confers strength and density on his cumulative experience.

Bellow is a slow writer. The novels have appeared at intervals of several years (1944, 1947, 1953, 1956, 1959, 1964, 1970, 1975 and 1982), each displaying a greater range, penetration, and breadth. The array of forms and the ends which these forms achieve are symptomatic of his protean craft. Each structural form contains its own creative juices, its own shaping, molding contours. Each structural experiment is an essential controller of the shape of the central consciousness; none exists for the sake of ornamentation. Bellow has tried a variety of architectural structures in his work. They range from the tight, highly controlled, subjective worlds of Joseph, Asa, and Tommy to the open-ended expansive inquiries of Augie, Henderson, and Herzog. Sammler's, Citrine's, and Corde's worlds rest at the very nexus of subjective brooding and outside interruption. In all cases, however, the structures serve as envelopes for the inner consciousness. The surface action, even when it is as diffuse and contradictory as it is in *Henderson* and *Augie March*, exists as a manifestation of the interior consciousness of the protagonist. Ways of seeing prefigure new ways of acting; new ways of acting, in turn, generate new ways of seeing. Bellow does more, however, than simply assert that "facts" are those sensations convincingly processed by the mind. Through the form of each individual work, the hero is led to assess his own thinking. The reader, at one further remove, is in an even more advantageous position. He or she can assess the assessment of the hero, noting its candor, its biases, its consistency.

Further, Bellow tends to alternate between a tight claustrophobic form like *The Victim* and an open-ended exploration like *Augie*. (Similarly, *Seize the Day* precedes *Henderson*, which is followed by *Herzog*, etc. One might protest that the expansive *Sammler* is followed by an even more expansive *Humboldt*; worth remembering in the total equation, however, is the taut, spare, nonfiction *To Jerusalem and Back*, 1976, which comes between the two.) This is hardly to suggest that Bellow is torn between portraying the virtues of the meditative man and demonstrating the effectiveness of the activist. Since all Bellow's forms serve to illuminate the interior life, the life where thought is action, I am persuaded that this alternation allows the author to drive different wedges in the reality of interior life. Sometimes the wedge creates a deep and narrow crevice, sometimes a gaping arena; the form is appropriate to the full inspection of whatever the artistic wedge uncovers; the two are, in fact, reciprocal.

In this light, *Dangling Man* presents to the reader a compulsive consciousness characterized in a terse, highly intellectualized journal. Joseph is confessing, looking for prayers of intercession or perhaps even acts of penance that will remove him from limbo. In his vault of a room, he tries to raise the ceiling of his consciousness and in so doing betrays all his prejudices, limitations, and hidden guilts. The structure of the novel, that of confessional journal, is one of printed imprisonment, a condition that parallels both the cultural situation and the mental persuasion of Joseph as he writes.

The Victim is a morality play where the forces of evil contend with the forces of good for the soul of Asa Leventhal. Allbee comes forth to summon Asa like a blue-eyed Bostonian specter, and his appearance triggers in Asa's mind a reckoning of his past, his good deeds and bad, his sins of commission and omission, his innocence or guilt. The cast of characters separates into those who speak for the good of Asa's soul (Schlossberg, Harkavy) and those who condemn him (Allbee, his anti-Semitic employers). He replies to the advances on both sides, alternately persuading them (and himself) of his guilt and innocence. The thrust of the form is toward awareness, toward the thoughtful rehearsal of Everyman's life, toward converting the aspects of that life found wanting into more significant ways of proceeding through the remainder of life.

Augie March is a robust picaresque, which takes a not too simple or naive rogue hero down the road of adventure and discovery. The movement is one of fluidity, an ongoing set of adventures, each one of which is stopped short of completion by Augie's "resistance." The message suggested, augmented, and supported by this form is that character is formed both by what it supports and by what it resists.

Seize the Day, Bellow's shortest and most compact work, is designed in its concentration of time, space, and action to deliver one sharp uppercut to the consciousness. If man cannot understand his purpose through years of thoughtful analysis, perhaps it is accessible to him through intensity of experience. The form is as spare as Tommy is flaccid and drives its nail of recognition directly into the heart.

In *Henderson* the hero receives blows everywhere else—to his Yankee ingenuity, his missionary spirit, his need for justice, his belief in miracle. The story is a series of rivets on the map of Africa, each affixed to Henderson's terrain, each attesting to a lesson learned, bungled, misapplied, or joyously understood. The result is a configuration as random as the rivets on a seventies blue-jeans jacket, worn with as much brash confidence and with about the same amount of utilitarian value.

Herzog's epistolary and flashback format expresses the mental Waterloo of the hero whose passionate and controlling intent is to write things down; disorder is unacceptable, yet all philosophical syntheses are suspect. The letters, therefore, while addressed to the famous as well as the obscure, are all written to Herzog himself, fragments of his disordered consciousness. One of the clearest indices to the relationship between form and idea emerges as the reader senses Herzog's recovery in terms of the cessation of letters.

Mr. Sammler's Planet is a novel of circles: circular consciousness, circular physical space, circular action. It is as rounded as the planet for which it speaks the epitaph; and its movements, involving spirals and vortices, suggest a wrapping up of progress, pain, and pleasure before man catapults off into a different world.

Humboldt's Gift is a novel of dizzying heights and depths: down into the steamy Russian baths in Chicago, up to skyscrapers; down into the grave, up to rarefied metaphysical heights.

The Dean's December uses two principles of alternation: the decay of both the East and the West; the heat of the crematorium and the cold of the stars. Common denominators connect both sets of opposites, just as Corde's consciousness sees sameness even in differentiation.

Thus, Bellow's narrative form is under constant change; it provides continually altering lenses on the reality the hero experiences as well as the consciousness through which that experience is filtered. As the world gets more and more peopled, and the social context more and more dense, the interior space in the hero's head expands. The narrow perceptions and prejudices of Joseph grow to encompass more and more until Artur Sammler has the most spacious planetary mind of all (and is grieving throughout the novel over a man whose brain is literally bursting). In like fashion, Bellow's art expands to accommodate and give full expression to the growing central consciousness. Joseph is an impressionist satisfied to record the sequence of images in his diary. Augie sees metaphors everywhere, one lesson suggests another, one acquaintance parallels another. Henderson, as the half-voluntary, half-impressed Rain King, is forced to view himself in a mythic context. Sammler must fight and finally accept his role as symbolic spokesman for his generation, just as Citrine wrestles with the prototype of the artist in America. Corde feels he has been sent "on a mission of observation and notation." It is the exfoliation of this internal space, mentally and artistically rendered, this exploration of the inner dome of man's mind that accounts for Bellow's changing narrative forms. Only exploration can accommodate humanity's incessant drive toward discovery.

The special quality of self-discovery that Bellow imparts to his heroes is achieved through the artistic manipulation of time, weight, and space. While time and space commonly characterize the world in which we live, weight is an ingredient of equal importance in the worlds Bellow's heroes occupy. The sheer weight of chaotic existence defines his characters. It expresses itself in the clutter of buildings, the press of people, the proliferation of choices, the abundance and turbulence of modern experience in which and through which the hero moves. Weighted by the density of modern life, Bellow's heroes are also pressed by the weight of their own personal failures and guilts. These image patterns are particularly appropriate to Bellow's portrayal of the central dilemma of modern man. Weight suggests the peculiar quality of being burdened by memories of the past, feelings of failure in the present, and anxiety about the future. Space is manipulated to define the cages the hero feels imprisoned within as well as to evoke his dreams of flight and escape. Time is of the greatest importance for Bellow's heroes, however, since it is their essential relationship to time and history that forms the foundations of their "contract" with the present. Time is at the crux of Bellow's art, since it is through the revitalized recognition of time and place that the novelist can, in Bellow's words, come to "create scale, to order experience, to give value, to make perspectives and to carry us toward sources of life, toward life-giving things."[3]

It seems almost too obvious to say that all Bellow's heroes are heavy men, dragging about with them not only a corporeal weight but a load of cares, anxieties, and burdens—which they seek unsuccessfully to jettison at every turn. Joseph broods that life is a "loathsome burden," and days drag by in weary, heavy succession. Asa feels "intolerably bound and compressed," his very presence a "great tiring weight." Despite Augie's "free" style and movement, he is weighted by family responsibilities, by others' convictions and value systems as symbolized by Einhorn, whom he carries on his back. Tommy Wilhelm can barely surface, he is so burdened: the "peculiar burden of his existence [lies] upon him like an accretion, a load, a hump." Henderson has a "pressure in the chest," his body is "one great weight." Herzog is "intolerably pressured, dragging around." Sammler almost succumbs, in a moment of panicky crowd pressure, to a heart attack. Indeed, when Henderson leaps and leaps and leaps; when, in suspended rapture, Augie watches the eagle fly; when Sammler dreams of the moon—any reader familiar with Bellow's world of pressures, burdens, and weights is transported. Flight, sheer rapturous weightlessness, is almost unheard of in Bellow's world and is uniformly temporary. The imagination can soar, as does Henderson's in Newfoundland and Herzog's in Ludeyville; the mind can take flight, as does Sammler's in his discussion with Dr. Lal. But the reality of man's existence is rooted in the here and now, in the pressures of the city, in the weights of family responsibility, in the obligations one feels to a man trying to meet death with dignity while ignoring the "screw in his neck." Flight can be seen only in terms of circles, in terms of where it comes to alight. Herzog flies from New York, only to alight in Chicago. His reality lies not in his escape but in his arrival. Similarly, weight can be measured only in terms of deliverance: from unnecessary guilt (Joseph), from revenge (Asa), from masochism (Tommy), from projection (Herzog). Weight and deliverance work in tandem to evoke the emotional texture of the lives of most of Bellow's heroes. It is only through their interanimation that the hero comes to "know what he knows."

Imagery associated with space and enclosure also triggers a sense of discovery in the hero. Most of Bellow's characters consider themselves imprisoned. In *Dangling Man*, Joseph is locked in his room. He, perhaps more than any succeeding Bellow protagonist, characterizes the view of modern history as a prison.

> I, in this room, separate, alienated, distrustful, find in my purpose not an open world, but a closed, hopeless jail. My perspectives end in the walls. Nothing of the future comes to me. Only the past, in its shabbiness and innocence. Some men seem to know exactly where their opportunities lie; they break

prisons and cross whole Siberias to pursue them. One room
holds me (92).

Bellow's heroes begin with the proposition, "I am burdened,
therefore I am,"[4] and must work from that essential component
of their identity. Since they feel jailed in this world, processing
their own information about the world through that set of
sensations, the world is characterized by images of rigid confinement: tombs, subways, hotel elevators, crowded and rig-
idly symmetrical city parks. As I suggested in the preceding
chapter, the interludes of idyllic fishing, rafting, hiking accessible to the American WASP imagination from Huck Finn to
Nick Adams are not available in Bellow's thickly populated
urban world. What *is* available is man's insatiable mind, and
the hero can never experience a condition of freedom until he
imagines it. Each protagonist, given his own points of departure, investigates how best to break the hermetic seal and imagine
a condition of freedom. Asa, for example, must learn to see the
world as something other than a condition of locked servitude.
When he rides the ferry to visit his brother's family, he thinks
only of the men locked in the engine room below, their bodies
straining to run the boat. When he visits the park with Philip,
he sees only cages; the movie is an "overcrowded dark tomb";
he bends to Allbee's accusation that Jews keep "their spirit
under lock and key"; and he is finally forced to characterize
himself as the "man in the mine who could smell smoke and
feel heat but never see the flames." By the end of the novel,
however, Asa has smelled smoke and clearly seen its source,
clearly rejected its intent. In refusing victimhood, Asa has
imagined other possibilities for his life. As the novel closes, he
is taking some steps toward realizing those possibilities.

There is a vital difference between imagining a condition of
freedom, predicated on what one knows already about his life,
and assuming that life is open-ended from the beginning. This
latter posture is the mistaken position Augie assumes when he
cheerfully announces he can enter all "rooms" (lives) and exit at
will; knock at all "doors" and expect them to open. There are
rooms that are impenetrable, he discovers, like the room in the

home for the blind where Mama is sent, the tiny rooming house toilet where Simon weeps uncontrollably, the degrading institution where Grandma Lausch spends her last days. Most of all, Augie discovers, one is always within "the walls of his being."

Tommy Wilhelm's existence is a study of enclosure, from his plunge downward in a hotel elevator into a city sunk metaphorically beneath the sea to the visits with his father in the "bowels of the hotel." Although Tommy struggles to keep "the waters of the earth" from rolling over him, he looks "like a man about to drown." There is no way out except through his recognition of the true terms of his character. Tommy's collapse in the darkened parlor before the coffin and his ensuing cry for the "heart's ultimate need" confirm the death of the deluded, striving self. His exit from self-laceration may prefigure an entrance to freedom. In a similar conclusion in *Humboldt's Gift*, though "Humboldt's flowers are aborted in the bulb" (462) during his lifetime, Citrine's discovery of crocuses at his grave suggests another flowering of his spirit.

Henderson has more resources at his command to attempt to escape imprisonment. From the octopus cage in the aquarium to the basement room in which he plays his mournful melodies, his life in America appears void of space. But in Africa he finds a tribe enslaved to primitive rituals, enslaved to a frog-infested cistern, dependent upon caging animals to study their "natures." Even Dahfu is kept captive by Amazon guards. Henderson discovers it is an inner spaciousness that is vital; and this recognition, coupled with its emotionally liberating legacies, sends him "leaping and leaping and leaping."

Herzog is far beyond these leaps of faith. Rejecting any "doctrine of theology and suffering," he sees his own entrapments as merely a "form of life," one which will paralyze those who cannot imagine anything other than its confines. While he speaks with proper contempt of "the commonplaces of the Wasteland outlook, the cheap mental stimulants of Alienation," he struggles with the incapacitation produced by his own real suffering. Oddly enough, Herzog confers the greatest perspective on his life through his capacity for humor. (Augie and

Henderson are great comic characters; however, they don't see themselves as funny.) It is in imagining himself as Sono's "perfumed baby" and Ramona's "trained bear"—shuffling about at Manhattan cocktail parties, costumed in a madras jacket and continental-cut trousers—that Herzog judges his own seductions and finds them comic. It is in imagining Gersbach's lectures on Yiddish poems as the product of the mind of a "bloody freemason" and Madeleine's much admired intellect as a "beautiful mixture of pure diamond and Woolworth glass" that Herzog opens the lid on his grief. What rushes out is self-laceration. What rushes in is a sense of proportion. Order may lie less in knowing the place in which things go than in knowing the size they should assume.

Sammler is the true artist of scale. Sighting through his one good eye, he takes the measure of everything that crosses his path. While trapped upon the planet (and caged within New York City, which contains yet another "cage": the small room where he prepares his meager breakfasts and works on his manuscript), he refuses to live a life narrowly constricted by his own special needs. Although not without his own prejudices (women, the young, the less than hygienic), he refuses to see the world as a grave. He dreams of flight, of spaciousness, of the interstellar leaps of the unpredictable mind. In allowing himself those flights of imagination, Sammler is at least as convinced by energy as he is by entropy. In a conclusion very similar to Sammler's, Corde ascends to the "bright vibrations" of the heavens: "Something parted, began to slide above them. Segments of the curved surface opened quickly, and let in the sky—first a clear piercing slice. . . . If this present motion were to go on, you would travel straight out. You would go up into the stars." It is this vision that acts as the counterbalance to the deterioration "down below."

Bellow's artistic manipulation of time is of vital importance in the evocation of the central consciousness. Time is expanded or contracted, elongated or concentrated, flashed forward or flashed back in order to express, mold, and vivify the sensations registering upon the protagonist. Joseph and Asa are caught in situations that imply a time limitation: Joseph awaits his draft call; Asa awaits Mary's return, his brother Max's return, and—later—the reappearances of Allbee. Each man's sense of the coercion of time is never far from affecting his consciousness and lends a special urgency to each undertaking, a special magnitude to every day's events. Augie and Henderson enjoy a deceptive sense of timelessness, which each of them comes to disavow in the final intensity of his search. Each is looking backward in time (Augie is retelling his history; Henderson is explaining his failures) as if through the humus of memory the present should bloom with meaning. Each is driven by the urgency of dwindling possiblities: both are aging, both have tried a lot of failing schemes and quests, both feel that time is running out. By having each protagonist narrate his past ultimately in the light of his precarious present, Bellow lends a sense of pitch and emotional intensity to each narrative.

Tommy's history is capsuled into a forty-eight-hour apocalypse—utterly seamless hours, so equal in the level of their emotional urgency that the reader is hardly aware of divisions. Tommy believes that this is all the time he has left to command, and his actions reflect that desperation. Sammler, too, is pressed by the notion that time is running out, not only for himself but for the planet. His driving curiosity to observe all there is and to analyze the minutest particulars of dress, habit, speech, and gesture bespeak not only the trained eye of a professional but the passionate cataloging of a life that will soon pass. His consuming concern is with how life will recreate itself, even while his emotional allegiances are very much "of his world."

Time, space, and weight combine, then, in their cumulative imagery to create in Bellow's fictive worlds both a sense of fixity (a reckoning) and a sense of transcendence (what the imagination can experience may be capable of conversion into "fact"). Man is neither determined nor free, neither solely rooted in his time and place nor cut free of his personal and social history. It is in the interplay between fixity and freedom that Bellow's protagonists win their balance. The balance shifts with the individual mind in the process of responding to and creating its world in any given novel. It is a process of constant contraction and expansion, constant freezing and thawing.

Mr. Sammler's Planet is Bellow's most thorough portrait of the organic relation between fixity and flux, between fact and imagination, between contraction and expansion. The name "Sammler" itself means "collector,"[5] and Sammler—who is the integral consciousness of the novel—collects opinions, impressions, confessions just as surely as Shula collects coupons, Wallace occupations, and Angela men. The novel itself is a collection of images detailed "at the end of an age" when the moonshot is about to open up interstellar space. Each image pattern finds its counterpart or its antithesis in another image. The novel, consequently, is a compendium of cross references. The weight of Sammler's age and the press of his environment find their antithesis in discussions with Dr. Lal about emerging life on the moon. The imprisoning subways, buses, and oppressive lecture rooms that yield Sammler's worst moments find their opposition in images of escape: fluid birdlike motion in the air. Sammler's remarkable insight with his one good eye is countered by his "blind eye"—his disdainful references to the radical young, whose males are "hairy, dirty, without style" and whose females have "a bad smell" (9). Indeed, Sammler is not an unchallengeable touchstone, since he uniformly denigrates all women and, while criticizing the "uniform" of the young, neglects to note his own costume: an impeccable suit, a furled umbrella, and precision-shined shoes. Sammler is not, as his family and friends try to make him, "a judge and a priest"; he is a man humanly believable in his weaknesses and strengths.

What is really remarkable about Sammler's world is the way time, space, and weight converge in the book's climactic finale. We witness less than three full days of Sammler's life, yet in that time we see a benefactor who is dying, a pickpocket who symbolizes the potency of evil and racial challenge, two difficult daughters who baffle their fathers (Shula and Angela), the vulnerability of philosophical explanations (the theft of Lal's manuscript, Sammler's aborted lecture), and the dangers of misguided radicalism (the activities and personalities of Feffer and Eisen). Amazingly, in Sammler's flight across town in a taxi to reach the dying Gruner (a trip counterpointing the historical and cosmic flights in the book), his path crosses them all. His consciousness is forced to absorb them all. Sammler prefers limit, duty, moderation, and control. But the exigencies of his special time and place thrust him through a succession of half-mad, violent streetside scenes, culminating in the tableau at the center of the city where all his friends and relatives converge. Feffer is fighting the black pickpocket, whose picture he has snapped for submission to *Look*. Hopelessly outmatched, Feffer is pinned against a bus in the middle of a growing circle of the curious. While Sammler watches in helpless frustration, Eisen materializes from the crowd, swinging his bag of iron Israeli medallions like a lethal weapon at the black man. The pickpocket circles Feffer; Eisen circles the black man; the impassive knot of observers rings them all. Sammler, immobilized by age and rage, sees them all "orbiting from a very different foreign center" (288), though one from which, it must be acknowledged, humanity is ready to exit. The scene is a moment of multiplying concentric circles ready to collapse into a vortex. It expresses Sammler's final descent into the hell of modernity prior to his acknowledgment of Gruner's timeless dignity.

The movement between fixity and freedom, between "fact" and what conditions the mind can imagine, is at the heart of Bellow's stylistic concerns. He is on record early as declaring his wish to steer between two kinds of American novels: the novel of information with its "exclusive interest in externals, things, process, and documentation," and the novel of sensibility in which "the intent of the writer is to pull us into an all-sufficient consciousness which he, the writer, governs absolutely."[6] His works are narrated by introspective, self-fastened men, yet they are grounded in the weight and feel and solidity of the worlds these men inhabit. They contain both the lyric possibilities of a James novel and the gritty reality of a Dreiser novel.

Fixity and flux become the dynamic of Bellow's last four works: the sprawling *Humboldt's Gift* (1975), which, like *Henderson the Rain King*, runs its protagonist over several continents only to bring him "home" to face the incontrovertible fact of death; *To Jerusalem and Back* (1977), a nonfiction odyssey that implies by its very title Bellow's need to come to terms with modern Israel; "A Silver Dish" (1978), the story of a son's desperate efforts to ward off the reality of his father's slow death; and *The Dean's December* (1982), a novel which oscillates between the realities of Iron Curtain Bucharest and inner-city Chicago.

Humboldt's Gift provides another clear example of the kind of complicated plot that epitomizes the protagonist's desire to fly from adversity and simultaneously seek the truth. As Keith Opdahl puts it, "Plot in Bellow is hard won, wrested from a confusing density and multiplicity of people, ideas, events, and sensations. It's so hard won that we might well claim that the struggle *is* the plot, as all the protagonists seek to move from the overwhelming richness of experience to some kind of peace and clarity."[7]

Like Sammler's, Charles Citrine's story suggests that the individual's life means something incapable of being defined in isolation. Not only is he embroiled in domestic squabbles with his former wife, distracted by his mistress's pressures to marry, obligated to attend his brother's open-heart surgery in Texas, and entrapped by the seamy underworld figures in Chicago, but his life is defined by the invasion of two other personalities. Von Humboldt Fleisher, a great boisterous poet whose radical verse in the thirties lured Citrine out of the Midwest, disintegrates before Charlie's eyes. Rinaldo Cantabile, who likes to think of himself as a big butter-and-egg man but who is in fact a small-time gangster, craves deference from a figure of Charlie's intellectuality and hounds him mercilessly. Each of these figures attempts to "instruct" Charlie, to imbue him with his particular and often peculiar view of life. While he cannot escape either one, neither will he endorse a single view of life. He questions the nature of love, the burdens and benefits of filial ties, the self-indulgences of art, and the myopia of history—all as a consequence of Humboldt's and Cantabile's unrelenting presence in his life. For Charlie, life cannot be systematized either by assimilation of another's view or by escape from the history we share with others.

Citrine is preoccupied with what he calls "my significant

dead" (9)—a preoccupation that links all of Bellow's protagonists in increasingly visible ways of transcending the obsession
of the code hero. Citrine's inquiry into the claims of death is
reproduced in several serious and several comic forms: the burial
of Citrine's father, the reburial of Humboldt, his mistress's
marriage to a mortician, the sharing of a birthplace with Hou-
dini, the ideas of Rudolf Steiner on reincarnation and immortality. In fact, the title of the novel suggests not only a tangible
bequest but an intangible legacy—Humboldt's voice from beyond the grave, which transcends the "fact" of death. Citrine's
personal struggles with the "death question" expand into questioning this century's entropic view of history. Charlie refuses
to accept what he calls "crisis history," which requires men like
his friend Humboldt to take the world with existential anguish
and feel obliged to suffer through it as nakedly as possible. He
argues that the "Wastelander view" deprives the imagination of
its power to make independent judgments. Instead, he wants
to endorse what he believes Americans of this century have
missed: "our minds have allowed themselves to be convinced
that there is no imaginative power to connect every individual
to the creation independently" (364). In failing to credit the
self with the full measure of possibility, modern man has capit-
ulated to a defensive view of history.

That defensive view—the domino theory of we-all-fall-down—
is the view Bellow fights in modern Jerusalem and back in
"Chicagoland." The central consequence of visiting Israel—
despite its wonderful civility and ancient culture—is this realization: "What you do know is that there is one fact of Jewish
life unchanged by the creation of a Jewish state. You cannot
take your right to live for granted. Others can; you cannot."[8]
To be a survivor is to be one who also deplores ignorance and
suffering. To be a survivor is to be one who condemns nihilism
as an appropriate response to life.

"What do you do about death?" Bellow asks in the opening
line of his beautifully crafted short story, "A Silver Dish." It is
a question that has appeared in multifoliate forms in the novels:
the death figure kisses Joseph; Allbee and Leventhal wrestle
before the gas oven; Augie is almost murdered by Bateshaw;

Tommy hemorrhages money; Henderson confronts the dying Dahfu; Herzog almost murders Gersbach; Sammler stands with the corpse of his beloved Gruner; Citrine deals with the death of Humboldt; Corde flies with his wife to the deathbed of her mother. Bellow's answer, as described in this paradigmatic story, is that you live life in all its rich and complex possibilities. A part of that rich experience includes for Woody Selbst an acknowledgment of his father's death:

> After a time, Pop's resistance ended. He subsided and subsided
> . . . Pop divided himself. And when he was separated from his
> warmth, he slipped into death.[9]

By observing his father's resistance and acquiescence, Selbst learns that one can neither pronounce absolute verdicts on life nor avoid the reality of death. For all of Bellow's protagonists, the message of death is to seek purpose in life.

The Dean's December attempts to decode the message of death and from it extract a new purpose for living. "Corde, who led the life of an executive in America—wasn't a college dean a kind of executive?—found himself six or seven thousand miles from his base, in Bucharest, in winter, shut up in an old-fashioned apartment. Here everyone was kind—family and friends, warmhearted people—he liked them very much, to him they were 'old Europe.' But they had their own intense business. This was no ordinary visit. His wife's mother was dying. Corde had come to give support" (1).

Caught in a situation he can neither control nor participate in fully, because of his foreigner's difficulty with the language and the facts of life in an Iron Curtain country, Albert Corde is like Artur Sammler—an observer of life, an estimator of its values, and a private philosopher. He has plenty of time to observe and plenty of pent up opinions for his interior monologues. While Sammler is an intellectual participant in a world of an order different from that of the New York he occupied, Corde has left his home in Chicago for Rumania in the middle of two alienating crises. As dean of students in his university, Corde has been involved in the investigation of the death of one

of his students. The investigation opens a seam in the simmer-
ing racial strife of the city, and the murder trial is in session
when Corde and his wife are called to his mother-in-law's
deathbed.

Simultaneously, Corde—a successful journalist before becoming dean—is in disfavor in Chicago because of a series of
highly critical articles he has written about the crime, racial
violence, and corruption in that city. The articles register the
same distillate of despair that characterized Sammler's observations a decade earlier.

Fixity and flux inform both the structure and the argument
in the novel. Corde is both "struck" and furiously kicking;
modern man is a product and simultaneously dismantling the
process. In 312 pages Bellow manages to set these inner and
outer structures in motion in both Chicago and Bucharest. But
unlike the final compelling scenes in *Mr. Sammler's Planet*, which
wrest the reader's attention away from Sammler's polemics and
rivet it upon one uncommon man's "contract with life," this
novel's appeal is wholly intellectual. The estimates of Corde—
and our own—about the world he inhabits are as gray and
autumnal as the dimly lit, freezing city of Bucharest, which
dominates the horizon. While Corde wants to recover "the
world that is buried under the debris of false description or
non-experience," the atmosphere the novel exudes is the "air-
sadness" Corde observes in Rumania:

> December brown set in at about three in the afternoon. By four
> it had climbed down the stucco of old walls, the gray of Com-
> munist residential blocks: brown darkness took over the pave-
> ments, and then came back again from the pavements more
> thickly and isolated the street lamps. These were feebly yellow
> in the impure melancholy winter effluence. Air-sadness, Corde
> called this. In the final stage of dusk, a brown sediment seemed
> to encircle the lamps. Then there was a livid death moment.
> Night began (*Dean's December*, 3).

If, as this chapter argues, Bellow's particular American gift
is organicism—the symbiosis of form and meaning—then surely
the strangely fatigued and frozen style of *The Dean's December* is

meant to convey the winter of life that is particularly appropriate in eastern Europe and in America's own brutalized cities. But when this abstract style appeared before—as it did in the endless monologues of Charles Citrine, and the diatribes of Sammler on modern life—it was held in balance by a counterforce, the exuberance of an imagination that cannot breathe "air-sadness" for too long before exploding into energized quests.

Narrative drive is also significantly reduced by funneling all of the conflicts in the novel through Corde's personality and speech. Unlike *Humboldt's Gift*, whose offstage personalities are at least as compelling as Citrine, *The Dean's December* wagers everything on its central character. Albert Corde, alone, must not only register the concrete world "so murderous and humanly meager," but also articulate a vision of a life that can replace or transcend this existence.

We might expect the conclusion to give us a glimpse of his vision—one akin to Henderson "leaping and leaping," to Sammler praying for the soul of Gruner, to Citrine seeing the first crocus blooms on the grave of Humboldt. And the attempt at ascendency is there; but it is curiously unconvincing, since it is yoked to Corde's wife—a figure he reveres, but whom we don't come to know very well. Minna, an astronomer of considerable reputation, has been allocated time with the Mount Palomar telescope. In the last scene of the novel, she and Corde ascend the tower to the dome that opens access for the telescope:

> And what he saw with his eyes was not even the real heavens. No, only white marks, bright vibrations, clouds of sky roe, tokens of the real thing, only as much as could be taken in through the distortions of the atmosphere. Through these distortions you saw objects, forms, partial realities. The rest was to be felt. And it wasn't only that you felt, but that you were drawn to feel and to penetrate further, as if you were being informed that what was spread over you had to do with your existence, down to the very blood and the crystal forms inside your bones. Rocks, trees, animals, men and women, these also drew you to penetrate further, under the distortions (comparable to the atmospheric ones, shadows within shadows), to find their real being with your own. This was the sense in which you were drawn (311).

This is another vision, one tied to the flights of imagination Sammler associated with the moonshot, but it comes through a character and a discipline so mysterious and secondary to Corde that it seems unable to survive the "descent." Minna and her scientist friends wear their insulated suits against the cold. "She waved to her husband, cheerful, and closed herself in. She was Corde's representative among those bright things so thick and close" (312).

Whatever difficulties in craft *The Dean's December* displays, it demonstrates undeniably Bellow's continuing effort to portray human beings caught in the middle of a spiritual crisis, overwhelmed by the stubborn fact of death and yet refusing to pronounce it as the last word. And while Albert Corde comes dangerously close to being the "reality instructor" that Bellow's earlier fiction undercuts, he also worries about the inadequacy and imprecision of all his theories. It is finally Corde's realization that he, and many of his compatriots, have lost the power to feel "the motion of the soul" that touches the reader.

What is particularly admirable in *The Dean's December* is Bellow's willingness to take on the "big questions"—the issues that make private consciousness and public conscience mirrors of each other. "Saul Bellow has gone public," one critic of *The Dean's December* reports, and this is risky business. When the author and his protagonist become synonymous and when artistic authority and moral authority unite, Bellow runs dangerously close to committing the error he ascribes to Hemingway. Authorial instruction, however, is not the impetus behind *The Dean's December*. Instead, the book attempts, in the tradition of Henry Adams, to discover the meaning of history. If the protagonist cannot find it in chronological sequence or in the lives of great men or in great theories, perhaps he can locate it in the story of his own life, transformed imaginatively and aesthetically. As does *The Education of Henry Adams*, Corde wants to expose relentlessly the fraudulent aspects of modern society and shock humanity into an awareness of its plight. And as does Adams's *Mont-Saint-Michel and Chartres*, Corde argues that humanity's sole dependence on fact and reason has been largely responsible for the fragmentation of the modern world. The individual has lost the capacity to feel, to revere, to love—a capacity that brings (in Adams's terms) "unity" out of "multiplicity."

What finally speaks in *The Dean's December* is not Corde's voice or Bellow's behind-the-scenes instruction. Instead, a daring conjunction of symbols provides another "way of knowing," an aesthetic one. Just as Adams opposed and united the cross and the railroad, the virgin and the dynamo, so Bellow opposes and unites the crematorium and the stars.

Corde's Rumanian ordeal culminates in Valeria's cremation. In a memorable scene that marks the emotional center of the book, Corde is asked to descend into the fiery crypt to identify the body and sign the death certificate before Valeria is committed to the furnace. Feeling himself "crawling between heaven and earth," Corde performs this, his last service, for Valeria.

> It was like a stokehold. It went into the tissues, drove all your moisture to the surface. Corde, who had come down shivering, now felt the hot weight of the fedora, his sweatband soaking. . . . There were other bodies preceding Valeria's. Corde could only think of her as the dead, waiting to be burned. As between frost and flames, weren't flames better? (213).

After the cremation, he comes up to join the funeral party once again.

> So, again the freezing dome and the crowd surrounding Minna. Better this cold than that heat. Corde's breast, as narrow as a ladder, was crowded with emotions—fire, death, suffocation, put into an icy hole or, instead, crackling in a furnace. Your last options. They still appeared equally terrible. How to choose between them! (214).

The fire and ice images, the lower "stokehold" and the "freezing dome" which in this passage suggest one's "last options," also figure in the heightened awareness Corde has of the centers of fire, the stars, and the Palomar dome that provides access to those stars.

> And because there was a dome, and the cold so absolute, he came inevitably back to the crematorium, *that* rounded top and its

huge circular floor, the feet of stiffs sticking through the curtains, the blasting heat underneath where they were disposed of, the killing cold when you returned and thought your head was being split by an ax. But that dome never opened. You could pass through only as smoke.

This Mount Palomar coldness was not to be compared to the cold of the death house. Here the living heavens looked as if they would take you in (310–11).

By employing these symbols, Bellow speaks to both our fear of termination and our hope for transcendence. In joining them, he asks that we see them as emanating from the same source. The symbols speak of human needs in ways more encompassing and persuasive than does the author as "spokesman." The aesthetic that Bellow creates in *The Dean's December* balances "the pangs of higher intuition" with "the muddy suck of the grave underfoot."

If it is true that fixity and freedom are at the heart of Bellow's conception of the human dilemma, it is equally true that all his works suggest the transforming powers of the imagination. As King Dahfu says, "The career of our species is evidence that one imagination after another grows literal. . . . Imagination! It converts to actual. It sustains, it alters, it redeems! . . . What Homo Sapiens imagines, he may slowly convert himself to" (*Henderson*, 271). While Bellow's heroes discover the dangers of being recruited into others' versions of the real, they are encouraged to realize their own imaginations, to imagine the conditions beyond those in which they are presently mired. Some critics see this as a wholly Jewish strain in Bellow's fiction. John Clayton puts the case persuasively:

How has the Jew said *Yes* in the face of the grimmest facts? Essentially, he has been conscious of the presence of an ideal world lying not outside but within the every-day world. The ideal world is not a heavenly Jerusalem but the earthly Jerusalem returned. . . . Heaven is this world redeemed. So while there is great tension between the world as it is and the world as it will be, both poles are immediately present.[10]

While the feeling that the world is sanctified is certainly trace-able to Jewish sources, it also possesses a considerable history in American writers' "legacy of wonder." The power of the imagination to be liberating and redemptive is behind Cooper's urgency to write an American novel, behind Hawthorne's con-ception of the romance, behind Melville's symbolic paralleling of the whale hunt with America's destiny. It is celebrated in Whitman's "Song of the Open Road," in Gatsby's green light, and in Dilsey's capacity to endure. In a very real sense, the conversion of imagination to reality triggered the discovery of America itself. Rather than relegating his fiction to a special category, Bellow's emphasis upon the transforming power of the imagination stamps his work with the indelible imprint of the American experiment. One of Bellow's central tenets is that life can proceed only as it renews itself; the imagination can triumph only as it finds new ways to realize itself.

Yet Bellow's celebration of freedom and his belief in the transforming power of the imagination are possible only when and as man comes to identify, to "fix" his place in both his personal and social history. The American imagination por-trayed by Bellow is not escapist. His heroes find no cessation of anxiety simply by lighting out for the Territory. Neither are they able to achieve peace in a willed divorce from society. Bellow's heroes do not confront the sacred emptiness of space that characterizes the outer terrain of Cooper and Melville's explorations, nor do they confront the exalted innocence, the belief—be it covert or overt—in an "orgiastic future" that characterizes the inner terrain of Fitzgerald's and Hemingway's explorations. Rather, they bring with them the weight of Eu-rope, the authority of their own personal and cultural history, a keen sense of the limits of social politics, and some precious fragments of conviction.

Bellow's fiction addresses itself to the problems of living in cultural modernism after ideal expectations have died and faith in "self-reliance" in its old sense of the "godly blessedness of human reach" (Irving Howe) has vanished as an innocent illu-sion. Since his heroes are never possessed of idyllic expecta-tions, they need not shore up defenses against "what has been lost." Since they have few unshakable assumptions about life, they have little need either to defend or to repudiate the values of a Puritan-isolationist past. They seek less to protect principles of value in the culture they inherit than to discover how to live meaningfully within the pattern of world experience.

Bellow's work, in its concentration upon history, social integration, and communal values, integrates the terms of the culture it inherits with the social and historical consciousness it brings as a gift to that culture. His fiction skirts the suffering-servant sentimentality that relegates the Jew to a position of specialness, precious in his capacity to suffer or sanctified in his capacity to hope. Nor does his work bespeak WASP utopias; it is not the fiction of limitless possibility that sets an initiate upon the open road, carrying on his back a kerchief full of Edenic dreams.

Bellow runs a tougher, more essential route than the assumptions of special-category fiction allow. His work portrays the dilemma of the modern hero caught in a history he must acknowledge, weighted by fears and anxieties he must quell by confrontation rather than evasion, and rooted in a time and place that he is required both to accept and to redeem. Bellow accepts Emerson's challenge to become "man thinking." At the same time, he transforms that injunction into a call for world awareness.

The old American yearnings are not gone. A belief in the perfectability of the individual, the notion of an accountable society, faith in the exercise of a rational intelligence, confidence in the regenerative capacity of human beings all figure prominently in Bellow's work. However, what enriches these grand visions is Bellow's distanced, lean, and argumentative consciousness. It insists on sensitivity to dangers extending to the whole of humanity. It urges sensitivity to social injustices, to failed utopias, and to a continuing shrinkage in the conditions for creative growth.

His is far from a cynic's prediction of the future. But he refuses his characters any long-term retreat into protective isolation or any minimizing of the problems that beset them as members of a society struggling for its moral existence. The blazing conviction in Bellow's fiction is that human beings can "know what they know" and in that knowledge can right their experience. Within this demanding conviction, Bellow continues to write novels that push out the perimeters of the American literary consciousness and enrich and expand our literary horizons.

Conclusion

Saul Bellow's novels insist on the possibility of "navigation by the great stars." Despite modern alienation, his protagonists retain their freedom to chart personal destinies which may afford, at any moment, a "glimpse of deep-water greatness."

In a scene from *Augie March*, Augie sees Trotsky step out of a small car in the cathedral square of a Mexican town. Down on his luck, having crawled "from one clam-rake to the next," Augie feels the internal movements of what Emerson calls "divine discontent":

> What it was about him that stirred me up was the instant impression he gave—no matter about the old heap he rode in or the peculiarity of his retinue—of navigation by the great stars, of the highest considerations, of being fit to speak the most important human words and universal terms. When you are as reduced to a different kind of navigation from this starry kind as I was and are only sculling on the shallow bay, crawling from one clam-rake to the next, it's stirring to have a glimpse of deep-water greatness. And, even more than an established, an exiled greatness, because the exile was a sign to me of persistence at the highest things (374).

In Bellow's world the cost of attaining vision beyond "the shallow bay" frequently amounts to exile—from the self and from the human community. But at the very least, his heroes summon the courage to look at the stars. To believe in the possibility of personal destiny is to share in the nineteenth-century romantic tradition that stresses the power of the human mind to overcome fragmentation and to grasp a unified and valuable human experience. Bellow shares Thoreau's and Emerson's insistence on informed thought: "the intellect is a cleaver; it discerns and rifts its way into the secret of things" (*Walden*). Inquiry and action are bound together for "man thinking":

"every man's condition is a solution in hieroglyphic to those inquiries he would put. He acts it as life, before he apprehends it as truth" (*Nature*).

While these characteristics are equally applicable to the English romantics like Keats and Wordsworth, whom Henderson quotes, they are packaged in a way peculiar to America.[1] The quests Asa and Tommy undertake for spiritual renewal are complicated by the need for material success. Equality of vision in America is yoked to equality of economic opportunity. The moral vision accessible to us all—the spiritual prong of the American Dream—has its materialistic counterpart: the acquisition of money, goods, and status. If, as popular Calvinist doctrine holds, the accumulation of worldly goods is a signal of God's blessing, then material success is a symptom of spiritual success. Thoreau is the first writer to separate these two tangled threads and suggest that acquisitiveness exacts a moral cost. The desperate price of confusing "character" with "status" registers its most harrowing effects in American naturalism: in Clyde Griffiths's version of "an American tragedy," or in McTeague's compulsive wrestling with gold.

The battle between moral authority as sanctification and material success as sanctification troubles Bellow's early "strivers." Recorders of their own experience, impaled on seemingly contradictory American Dreams, they cry out, "I want, I want," in an effort to acquire more than goods or justification. Like Sister Carrie's spiraling consciousness, their dreams are of what they cannot as yet enact, though dreaming is the vital precondition to achieving. Both romanticism and naturalism summon them to "see rightly."

If the quest is a means of identifying moral choice and acting ethically as a consequence, "how to know" is the necessary second step—requiring both separation and reengagement. The pattern of withdrawal and reentry into communal experience is also predominantly, though not exclusively, American in its expression. The significance of solitude—its promise and its terror—emerges from the colonial literature of new settlements. When William Bradford remarks that "half the company died that winter" or Anne Bradstreet writes instructions to her surviving children prior to the birth of her sixth child, we become acutely aware of the precariousness of any one life, of the sparsely populated reaches of this country, and of the incalculable value of companionship. Romantic literature separates the one from the many as an important prerequisite to self-knowledge. American naturalism, on the other hand, pictures the urban reality of nineteenth- and twentieth-century America, where one may still be "in solitary." Dreiser's Chicago—with its press of people, crowded restaurants, insides of hotel rooms and cheap boardinghouses—conditions the backdrop for Bellow's novels. Yet his heroes withdraw both as an unconscious consequence of this pressure and simultaneously as a conscious romantic choice in order to acquire healing insight. Double impulses also prompt their returns: they *choose* to return because, like Thoreau, they "have other lives to live"; they *must* come back or they will suffer the fate of the forgotten Hurstwood, standing with all the other faceless men in the soup line. In *Henderson* and in *Herzog*, Bellow draws from both romantic and naturalist traditions in American literature to suggest that knowing emerges out of connections to human experience larger than the solitary self.

This larger fate motivates Bellow's later questers: Sammler, Citrine, and Corde. Their view is reflexive; it brings focus to America through more cosmopolitan experience. Sammler is a European Jew and a survivor of the Holocaust; Citrine is a "winner of the big awards" and "world class" as a thinker; and Corde is for some time an international journalist based in Paris. As detached and civilized observers, they bring powers of attentiveness and discrimination to bear on America. In the tradition of Henry James, assessments arise from their ability to juxtapose cultures, histories, and value systems. They bear a further yoke with James's protagonists: despite intellectual distance, each holds a vital stake in the outcome of his assessments. Critical detachment is counterbalanced by passionate concern.

This passionate concern for others, and for issues larger than the "merely personal," marks Bellow's novels with a "persistence at the highest things." This ultimate concern has analogues, both positive and negative, in earlier American literature. Even within a tradition of orphanhood and exile, it prompts Ishmael to announce that we are all part of "a joint stock-company," and it causes the reclusive Hawthorne protagonist to rejoin "the magnetic chain of humanity." It resounds exuberantly in Whitman's voyaging voice: "One's self I sing, a simple, separate person, / yet utter the word Democratic, the word En-Masse." In reverse fashion, it speaks hauntingly of the failure of human connections in the sheer survival tactics of Stephen Crane's "Blue Hotel" and "The Monster," and in the protective cynicism of Ernest Hemingway's "The Killers" and "A Clean Well-Lighted Place." If we believe with Henry Adams that modern man's alienation is posited not on his failure to think precisely but on his failure to feel expansively, then Bellow's synthesis of reason and passionate concern is the antidote to isolation.

Bellow's antidote fuses oppositions through the process of art. He overcomes isolation through the telling of the story. His style and his aesthetic speak more powerfully than any authorial instruction. His art is composed of two highly distinctive elements: an elevated tone that Martin Amis calls the "High Style," and an informing set of symbols that extend meaning beyond "message."

> The High Style attempts to speak for the whole of mankind,
> with suasion, to remind us of what we once knew and have since
> forgotten or stopped trying to regrasp. . . . Humboldt suffered
> from "the longing for passionate speech." Corde, like Sammler,
> aches to deliver his "inspired recitation." It is the desire to speak,
> to warn—to *move*, above all.[2]

Bellow's desire to alert us, to put us on notice, echoes Emerson's intention in "The American Scholar": "We will walk on our own feet, we will work with our own hands; we will speak our own minds. The study of letters shall be no longer a name for pity, for doubt, and for sensual indulgence. The dread of man and the love of man shall be a wall of defence [*sic*] and a wreath of joy around all." The "study of letters" is the highest form of "navigation."

The symbols that speak beyond the messages in any given Bellow novel are sometimes coded in confrontations with natural creatures in the manner of the white whale: Caligula the eagle, or Atti the lion. Sometimes they are the consequence of a moment of symbolic confrontation in the manner of the scarlet letter: Tommy weeping at the coffin of a stranger, Sammler cornered by the black pickpocket, Corde descending into the fire and ice of the crematorium. They move beyond exactness of statement or precise definition, and remain shimmering in the memory long after the particulars of plot are gone. They constitute what Hugh Kenner calls the "high Saul Bellow moment."[3] A memorable epiphany of this sort comes near the end of the fabulist adventures of Henderson, when the hero climbs into a roller coaster with a mangy old trained circus bear, Smolak, now too old to ride his bike anymore.

> And while we climbed and dipped and swooped and swerved and rose again higher than the Ferris wheels and fell, we held on to each other. By a common bond of despair we embraced, cheek to cheek. . . . I was pressed into his long-suffering, age-worn, tragic, and discolored coat as he grunted and cried to me (338).

These moments of symbolic confrontation are devoid of reflections. Instead, they prompt readers to explore their extended meanings. They ask us to be discoverers, too, our own "sort of Columbus."

My effort to relate Bellow to an American tradition of vision, moral allegory, and symbolic discovery does not deny the influence of Russian novelists like Dostoevsky, whom Bellow credits with giving him the "plot germ" for *Dangling Man* and *The Victim*. Nor does it dispute the special riches of the Jewish tradition so amply documented since Bellow's star began to rise. Rather, it attempts to address what Bellow might have meant when asked about his roots. He replied, "As a child I took home Dreiser, Twain, and Sherwood Anderson, not the wisdom of Maimonides."[4] In a recent interview, he characterized himself in this way: "I think of myself as an American of Jewish heritage. All we [Malamud, Roth, Bellow] wanted was to add ourselves to the thriving enterprise we loved."[5]

Saul Bellow not only added his voice to the "thriving enter-prise" but also helped to cultivate a new world for American fiction. His "underground man" eventually came above ground to see, to connect with, and to believe in a future for the world he inhabits.

Notes

Introduction

1. Bellow, "Writer as Moralist," 62.
2. Bellow, "Recent American Fiction," 7.
3. Quoted in Epstein, "Saul Bellow of Chicago," 6.
4. Ibid.
5. Saul Bellow, "Bellow on Himself and America," *The Jerusalem Post Magazine*, 3 July 1970, 12.
6. Jackson J. Benson, "An Introduction: Bernard Malamud and the Haunting of America" in *The Fiction of Bernard Malamud* (Corvallis: Oregon State University Press), 21.
7. Quoted in Harper, *Desperate Faith*, 63.
8. Quoted in Klein, *After Alienation*, 70.
9. Leslie Field, "Introduction," *Modern Fiction Studies* (Special Bellow Issue), 3.
10. Kulshrestha, *Saul Bellow*, 15.
11. Field, *Modern Fiction Studies* (Special Bellow Issue), 10.

Chapter One: The Health of the Eye

1. Saul Bellow, "Two Morning Monologues," *Partisan Review* 8 (May-June 1941): 233. All subsequent quotations will be cited in the text from this edition.
2. Saul Bellow, *The Adventures of Augie March* (New York: Viking, 1953), 434. All subsequent quotations will be cited in the text from this edition.
3. Saul Bellow, *Henderson the Rain King* (New York: Viking, 1959), 275. All subsequent quotations will be cited in the text from this edition.
4. Saul Bellow, *Dangling Man* (New York: Vanguard, 1944), 24–26. All subsequent quotations will be cited in the text from this edition.
5. Saul Bellow, *The Victim* (New York: Vanguard, 1947), 232. All subsequent quotations will be cited in the text from this edition.

6. A number of critics have suggested the *doppelgänger* motif in *The Victim*, most notably Baumbach (*Landscape of Nightmare*, 35–54).
7. Saul Bellow, *Seize the Day* (New York: Fawcett, 1965), 8. All subsequent quotations will be cited in the text from this edition.
8. Opdahl, Clayton, and Porter have all investigated the drowning and rebirth imagery in *Seize the Day*. The use of water imagery is detailed in Trowbridge, "Water Imagery," 62–73.
9. This is Clayton's useful phrase (*Saul Bellow*, 135).
10. Saul Bellow, *Henderson the Rain King* (New York: Viking, 1959), 112. All subsequent quotations will be cited in the text from this edition.
11. Saul Bellow, *Herzog* (New York: Viking, 1964), 29. All subsequent quotations will be cited in the text from this edition.
12. Saul Bellow, *Mr. Sammler's Planet* (New York: Viking, 1969), 33. All subsequent quotations will be cited in the text from this edition.
13. Saul Bellow, *Humboldt's Gift* (New York: Viking, 1975), 347. All subsequent quotations will be cited in the text from this edition.
14. Saul Bellow, *The Dean's December* (New York: Harper and Row, 1982), 1. All subsequent quotations will be cited in the text from this edition.
15. Quoted from an interview with Bernard Malamud in Joseph Wershba, "Not Horror but Sadness," *New York Post*, 14 September 1958, M2.
16. Bellow, "Writer as Moralist," 62.

Chapter Two: Retreat and Reentry

1. A number of critics have treated this archetypal pattern in American literature. Those who see its physical or psychological manifestations in Bellow's work include Fiedler, Geismar, Guttmann, Hassan.
2. Quoted in Hassan, *Radical Innocence*, 294.
3. Tanner, *City of Words*, 436.
4. Opdahl, *Novels of Saul Bellow*, 10.
5. Ibid., 51.
6. Saul Bellow, "The University as a Villain," *Nation* 185 (November 16, 1957): 362.
7. Irving Howe was the first critic to center on the bathing scene in *Herzog* as a turning point in the novel. Howe, Malin, and Kazin suggest that despite the grotesqueness of Gersbach's char-

acter, his act is an act of love, a holy act, performed on his knees. My interest is in Herzog as the *witness* to this act.

8. Saul Bellow, "Nobel Prize Address," *The American Scholar* 46 (Summer 1977): 325.

Chapter Three: Reality Instructors

1. Fiedler develops this idea at some length ("Saul Bellow," 103–10).
2. Clayton, *Saul Bellow*, 273–74.
3. Augie's phrase.
4. Harper, *Desperate Faith*, 60. Hassan (*Radical Innocence*) also has a useful section on reality instructors, separating them into two groups: benevolent con men, and malicious or misguided tricksters.
5. Bellow, "Recent American Fiction," 22–29. Bellow addresses himself to this question in the *Paris Review* interview with Gordon L. Harper, when he says, "I am quite prepared to admit that being habitual liars and self-deluders, we have good cause to fear the truth, but I'm not at all ready to stop hoping" (see Gordon L. Harper, "Saul Bellow, the Art of Fiction: An Interview," *Paris Review* 37 [Winter 1965]: 48–73).
6. Bruce J. Borrus, "Bellow's Critique of the Intellect," *Modern Fiction Studies* (Special Bellow Issue), 29–30.

Chapter Four: A Separate Peace

1. Benson, *Hemingway*, 3.
2. That Henderson is a parody of the Hemingway code hero is evident to any sensitive reader and has been admitted by Bellow himself. He suggests, "Hemingway has an intense desire to impose his version of the thing upon us, to create an image of manhood, to define the manner of baptism and communion." ("Hemingway and the Image of Man"). Critics like Ronald Lycette see Bellow's repudiation of Hemingway as consisting of a reaction against *macho*, a repudiation of hardboildom. Others, like Donald Markos, see Henderson's symbolic death and rebirth paralleling an archetypal pattern in Hemingway's fiction. The central problem in both Hemingway's and Bellow's fiction is how to channel one's energies correctly, how to act responsibly. While Hemingway's fiction concentrates upon the terms of that action, Bellow's fiction asks, "What does it *mean* to act responsibly?"

3. Bellow, "Hemingway and the Image of Man," 338–39.
4. Ibid.
5. Clayton catalogues a similar set of psychic defenses (*Saul Bellow*, 235). I am more indebted for these ideas to Moses Herzog, who discusses each of them at some length.
6. Sanderson, *Ernest Hemingway*, 41.
7. Bellow, "A Father-to-Be," *Mosby's Memoirs*, 146.
8. Ibid., 147.
9. Ibid., 150.
10. Carlos Baker, *Hemingway: The Writer as Artist* (Princeton: Princeton University Press, 1952), 102.
11. Ernest Hemingway, "Indian Camp," *The Nick Adams Stories* (New York: Charles Scribner's Sons, 1972), 18.
12. Ernest Hemingway, *The Old Man and the Sea* (New York: Charles Scribner's Sons, 1952), 9.
13. This is developed in the *Paris Review* interview, where Bellow is quoted as saying, "There are many skeptical, rebellious or simply nervous writers all around us, who, having existed a full twenty or thirty years in this universe, denounce or reject life because it fails to meet their standards as philosophical intellectuals. It seems to me that they can never know enough about it for confident denial. The mystery is too great. So when they knock at the door of mystery with the knuckles of cognition it is quite right that the door should open and some mysterious power should squirt them in the eye" (Gordon L. Harper, "Saul Bellow, the Art of Fiction: An Interview," *Paris Review* 37 [Winter 1965]: 65).
14. Quoted in Clayton, *Saul Bellow*, 245.
15. Ernest Hemingway, *A Farewell to Arms* (New York: Charles Scribner's Sons, 1929), 327.
16. Quoted in Gordon L. Harper, "Saul Bellow," 65.

Chapter Five: Technique as Discovery

1. Helen Weinberg posits a useful thesis on the relationship between Bellow's art and his ideas (*New Novel in America*, 40). She contends that "Bellow would repudiate any systematized findings, even the modern ones of existentialism. . . . Commitments are far more rudimentary [in his fiction] than any 'position' or intellectual attitude might imply."
2. Bellow, "Where Do We Go from Here," in *Saul Bellow and the Critics*, ed. Irving Malin (New York: New York University Press, 1967), 220.

3. For further information on Bellow's image patterns, see Malin, "Seven Images" in *Saul Bellow and the Critics*, 142–175.

4. Solotaroff, *Red Hot Vacuum*, 28.

5. Galloway, "*Mr. Sammler's Planet*: Bellow's Failure of Nerve," 19.

6. "The Distractions of the Fiction Writer," in *The Living Novel*, ed. Granville Hicks (New York: Macmillan, 1957), 298.

7. Keith Opdahl, "Stillness in the Midst of Chaos: Plot in the Novels of Saul Bellow," *Modern Fiction Studies* (Special Bellow Issue), 17.

8. Bellow, *To Jerusalem and Back*, 125.

9. Bellow, "A Silver Dish," 40, 62.

10. Clayton, *Saul Bellow*, 31.

Conclusion

1. Chavkin ("Bellow's Alternative to the Wasteland," 326–37) discusses Bellow in relation to the English romantic tradition, concentrating on Wordsworth.

2. Amis, "The Moronic Inferno," 5.

3. Hugh Kenner, "From Lower Bellowvia," *Harper's*, February 1982, 65.

4. *Pittsburgh Post-Gazette*, 11 April 1979, 7.

5. *New York Times Book Review*, 13 December 1981, 29.

Bibliography

Adler, Sidney. "The Image of the Jew in the American Novel." *Bulletin of Bibliography* 23 (September-December 1962): 211–13.

Aldridge, John W. "Nothing Left to Do but Think: Saul Bellow"; "The Complacency of Herzog." In *Time to Murder and Create: The Contemporary Novel in Crisis*, 87–94, 133–38. New York: David McKay, 1966.

Allen, Michael. "Idiomatic Language in Two Novels by Saul Bellow." *Journal of American Studies* 1 (October 1967): 275–80.

Allen, Walter. "War and Post War America." In *The Modern Novel in Britain and the United States*, 293–332. New York: E. P. Dutton, 1964.

Alter, Robert. "Sentimentalizing the Jews." *Commentary* 40 (September 1965): 71–75.

————. "Saul Bellow: A Dissent from Modernism." In *After the Tradition: Essays on Modern Jewish Writing*, 95–115. New York: E. P. Dutton, 1969.

————. *America and Israel: Literary and Intellectual Trends*. New York: Hadassah Education Series, 1970.

Amis, Martin. "The Moronic Inferno." *London Review of Books*, April 1982, 3–5.

Axthelem, Peter M. "The Full Perception: Bellow." In *The Modern Confessional Novel*, 128–77. New Haven: Yale University Press, 1967.

Baim, Joseph. "Escape from Intellection: Saul Bellow's Dangling Man." *University Review* 37 (Autumn 1970): 28–34.

————. "Henderson and the Rain King: A Major Theme and a Technical Problem." In *A Modern Miscellany*, edited by David P. Demarest, Jr., Lois S. Lamdin, and Joseph Baim, 53–63. Pittsburgh: Carnegie-Mellon University, 1970.

Baker, Carlos. *Hemingway: The Writer as Artist*. Princeton: Princeton University Press, 1952.

Baker, Sheridan. "Saul Bellow's Bout with Chivalry." *Criticism* 9 (Spring 1967): 109–22.

Balakian, Nona, and Charles Simmons, eds. *The Creative Present: Notes on Contemporary American Fiction.* Garden City, N.Y.: Doubleday, 1963.

Baruch, Franklin R. "Bellow and Milton: Professor Herzog in His Garden." *Critique* 9, no. 3 (1967): 74–83.

Baumbach, Jonathan. "The Double Vision: *The Victim* by Saul Bellow." In *The Landscape of Nightmare: Studies in the Contemporary American Novel,* 35–44. New York: New York University Press, 1965.

Bellow, Saul. "Two Morning Monologues." *Partisan Review* 8 (May-June 1941): 230–36.

———. *Dangling Man.* New York: Vanguard, 1944.

———. *The Victim.* New York: Vanguard, 1947.

———. *The Adventures of Augie March.* New York: Viking, 1953.

———. "Hemingway and the Image of Man." *Partisan Review* 20 (May-June 1953): 338–42.

———. *Seize the Day.* New York: Viking, 1956.

———. "The University as a Villain." *Nation* 185 (16 November 1957): 362.

———. *Henderson the Rain King.* New York: Viking, 1959.

———. *Herzog.* New York: Viking, 1964.

———. "Where Do We Go from Here? The Future of Fiction." *Michigan Quarterly Review* 1 (Winter 1962): 27–33.

———. "Recent American Fiction." Gertrude Clarke Whittal Poetry and Literature Fund Lecture. Washington: Library of Congress, 1963.

———. "The Writer as Moralist." *Atlantic Monthly* 211 (March 1963): 58–62.

———. *Mosby's Memoirs.* New York: Fawcett, 1969.

———. "Bellow on Himself and America." *The Jerusalem Post Magazine,* 13 July 1970, 12.

———. *Mr. Sammler's Planet.* New York: Viking, 1970.

———. *Humboldt's Gift.* New York: Viking, 1975.

———. *To Jerusalem and Back.* New York: Viking, 1976.

———. "A Silver Dish." *New Yorker,* 25 September 1978, 40–50.

———. *The Dean's December.* New York: Harper and Row, 1982.

Benson, Jackson. *Hemingway: The Writer's Art of Self Defense.* Minneapolis: University of Minnesota Press, 1969.

Bezanker, Abraham. "The Odyssey of Saul Bellow." *Yale Review* 57 (Spring 1969): 359–71.

Boulgar, James D. "Puritan Allegory in Four Modern Novels." *Thought* 44 (1969): 413–32.

Bradbury, Malcolm. "Saul Bellow's *The Victim*." *Critical Quarterly* 5 (Summer 1963): 119–28.

———. "Saul Bellow and the Naturalist Tradition." *Review of English Literature* (Leeds) 4 (October 1963): 80–92.

———. "Saul Bellow's Herzog." *Critical Quarterly* 7 (Autumn 1965): 269–78.

Bryant, Jerry H. "The Open Decision." In *The Contemporary American Novel and Its Intellectual Background*, 341–69. New York: Free Press, 1970.

Buchen, Irving H. "Jewish-American Writers as a Literary Group." *Renascence* 19 (Spring 1967): 142–50.

Burgess, Anthony. "The Postwar American Novel: A View from the Periphery." *American Scholar* 35, no. 1 (Winter 1965–1966): 150–56.

Campbell, Jeff H. "Bellow's Intimations of Immortality: *Henderson the Rain King*." *Studies in the Novel* 1 (Fall 1969): 323–33.

Chapman, Abraham. "The Image of Man as Portrayed by Saul Bellow." *College Language Association Journal* 10 (June 1967): 285–98.

Charles, Gerda. "Elizabethan Age of Modern Jewish Literature, 1950–1960: Decade of the Great Breakthrough." *World Jewry* 4 (September 1961): 15–17.

Chase, Richard. "The Adventures of Saul Bellow: Progress of a Novelist." *Commentary* 27 (April 1957): 323–30.

Chavkin, Allan. "Bellow's Alternative to the Wasteland: Romantic Theme and Form in *Herzog*." *Studies in the Novel* 3 (Fall 1979): 326–37.

Clay, George R. "The Jewish Hero in American Fiction." *Reporter* 17 (September 19, 1957): 43–46.

———. "The Creative Writer as a Jew." *Congress Bi-Weekly* 30 (September 16, 1963): 42–59.

Clayton, John Jacob. *Saul Bellow: In Defense of Man*. Rev. ed. Bloomington: Indiana University Press, 1979.

Crozier, Robert D. "Theme in *Augie March*." *Critique* 7 (Spring-Summer 1965): 18–32.

Demarest, David P., Jr. "The Theme of Discontinuity in Saul Bellow's Fiction: 'Looking for Mr. Green' and 'A Father-to-Be.'" *Studies in Short Fiction* 6 (Winter 1969): 175–86.

DeMott, Benjamin. "Jewish Writers in America." *Commentary* 39 (February 1961): 127–34.

Detweiler, Robert. "Patterns of Rebirth in *Henderson the Rain King*." *Modern Fiction Studies* 12 (Winter 1966–1967): 404–14.

————. *Saul Bellow: A Critical Essay*. Grand Rapids, Mich.: W. B. Eerdmans, 1967.

Dutton, Robert R. *Saul Bellow*. New York: Twayne, 1971.

Eisinger, Chester E. "Saul Bellow: Man Alive, Sustained by Love." In *Fiction of the Forties*, 341–62. Chicago: University of Chicago Press, 1963.

Epstein, Joseph. "Saul Bellow of Chicago." *New York Times Book Review*, 9 May 1971, 4, 12, 14, 16.

Feinstein, Herbert. "Contemporary American Fiction: Harvey Swados and Leslie Fiedler." *Wisconsin Studies in Contemporary Literature* 2 (Winter 1961): 79–98. (Two interviews which include discussions of Mailer, Bellow, Roth, West, and others.)

Fiedler, Leslie. *An End to Innocence: Essays on Culture and Politics*. Boston: Beacon, 1955.

————. "Saul Bellow." *Prairie Schooner* 31 (Summer 1957): 103–10.

————. "The Breakthrough: The American Jewish Novelist and the Fictional Image of the Jew." *Midstream* 4 (Winter 1958): 15–35.

————. *The Jew in the American Novel*. New York: Herzl Press, 1959.

————. *No! in Thunder: Essays on Myth and Literature*. Boston: Beacon, 1960.

————. "The Jew as Mythic American." *Ramparts* 2 (Autumn 1963): 32–48.

————. *Waiting for the End*. New York: Stein and Day, 1964.

Fineman, Irving. "The Image of the Jew in Our Fiction." *Tradition* 9 (Winter 1966): 19–47.

————. "The Image of the Jew in Fiction of the Future." *National Jewish Monthly* 82 (December 1967): 48–51.

Finkelstein, Sidney. "Lost Social Convictions and Existentialism: Arthur Miller and Saul Bellow." In *Existentialism and Alienation in American Literature*, 252–69. New York: International Publishers, 1965.

Fisch, Harold. "The Hero as Jew: Reflections on *Herzog*." *Judaism* 17 (Winter 1968): 42–54.

Fossum, Robert H. "The Devil and Saul Bellow." *Comparative Literature Studies* 3, no. 2 (1966): 197–206.

————. "Inflationary Trends in the Criticism of Fiction: Four Studies of Saul Bellow." *Studies in the Novel* 2 (1970): 99–104.

Freedman, Ralph. "Saul Bellow: The Illusion of Environment." *Wisconsin Studies in Contemporary Literature* 1 (Winter 1960): 50–65.

Freedman, William. "American Jewish Fiction: So What's the Big Deal?" *Chicago Review* 19, no. 1 (1966): 90–107.

Friedman, A. W. "The Jew's Complaint in Recent American Fiction: Beyond Exodus and Still in the Wilderness." *Southern Review* 8 (1972): 41–59.

Frohock, W. M. "Saul Bellow and His Penitent Picaro." *Southwest Review* 53 (Winter 1968): 36–44.

Galloway, David D. "Moses-Bloom-Herzog: Bellow's Everyman." *Southern Review* 2 (January 1966): 61–76.

————. *The Absurd Hero in American Fiction: Updike, Styron, Bellow, Salinger.* Rev. ed. Austin: University of Texas Press, 1970.

————. *"Mr. Sammler's Planet*: Bellow's Failure of Nerve." *Modern Fiction Studies* 19 (Spring 1975): 17–29.

Geismar, Maxwell. "The Jewish Heritage in Contemporary American Fiction." *Ramparts* 2 (Autumn 1963): 5–13.

————. "Saul Bellow: Novelist of the Intellectuals." In *American Moderns: From Rebellion to Conformity*, 210–24. New York: Hill and Wang, 1971.

Glicksberg, Charles I. "A Jewish American Literature?" *Southwest Review* 53 (Spring 1968): 196–205.

Goldberg, Gerald Jay. "Life's Customer: Augie March." *Critique* 3 (Summer 1960): 15–27.

Goldfinch, Michael A. "A Journey to the Interior." *English Studies* 43 (October 1962): 439–43.

Gross, Theodore L. "Saul Bellow: The Victim and the Hero." In *The Heroic Ideal in American Literature*, 243–61. New York: Free Press, 1971.

Guerard, Albert J. "Saul Bellow and the Activists: On *The Adventures of Augie March.*" *Southern Review* 3 (July 1967): 528–96.

Guttmann, Allen. "Jewish Radicals, Jewish Writers." *American Scholar* 32 (Autumn 1963): 563–75.

————. "The Conversions of the Jews." *Wisconsin Studies in Contemporary Literature* 6 (Summer 1965): 161–76.

————. *The Jewish Writer in America: Assimilation and the Crisis of Identity.* New York: Oxford University Press, 1971.

Hall, James. "Portrait of the Artist as a Self-Creating, Self-Vindicating, High-Energy Man." In *Lunatic Giant in the Drawing Room: The British and American Novel since 1930*, 127–80. Bloomington: Indiana University Press, 1968.

Handy, William J. "Saul Bellow and the Naturalistic Hero." *Texas Studies in Literature and Language* 5 (Winter 1964): 538–45.

Harper, Gordon Lloyd. "Saul Bellow." In *Writers at Work: The "Paris Review" Interviews*, 3rd ser., 175–96. New York: Viking, 1967.

Harper, Howard M., Jr. "Saul Bellow: The Heart's Ultimate Need." In *Desperate Faith: A Study of Bellow, Salinger, Mailer, Baldwin, and*

Updike, 7–64. Chapel Hill: University of North Carolina Press, 1967.

―――. "Trends in Recent American Fiction." *Contemporary Literature* 12 (1971): 204–29.

Harris, Mark. *Saul Bellow: Drumlin Woodchuck*. Athens: University of Georgia Press, 1980.

Hassan, Ihab. "Saul Bellow: The Quest and Affirmation of Reality." In *Radical Innocence: Studies in the Contemporary American Novel*, 290–324. Princeton: Princeton University Press, 1961.

Hays, Peter. *The Limping Hero: Grotesques in Literature*. New York: New York University Press, 1971.

Hicks, Granville. "A Matter of Critical Opinion." *Saturday Review* 48 (7 August 1965): 19–20.

―――. "Saul Bellow." In *Literary Horizons: A Quarter Century of American Fiction*, 49–63. New York: New York University Press, 1970.

Hoffman, Michael J. "From Cohn to Herzog." *Yale Review* 58 (Spring 1969): 342–58.

Howard, Jane. "Mr. Bellow Considers His Planet." *Life* 68 (3 April 1970): 57–60.

Howe, Irving. "Mass Society and Post-Modern Fiction." *Partisan Review* 26 (Summer 1959): 420–36.

Hughes, Daniel J. "Reality and the Hero: *Lolita* and *Henderson the Rain King*." *Modern Fiction Studies* 6 (Winter 1960–1961): 345–64.

Hull, Bryon D. "*Henderson the Rain King* and William James." *Criticism* 13 (Fall 1971): 402–14.

Jones, David R. "The Disappointment of Maturity: Bellow's *The Adventures of Augie March*." In *The Fifties: Fiction, Poetry, Drama*, edited by Warren French, 83–92. Deland, Fla.: Everett/Edwards, 1971.

Josipovici, Gabriel. "Bellow and Herzog." *Encounter* 37 (November 1971): 49–55.

Kakutani, Michiko. "A Talk with Saul Bellow." *New York Times Book Review*, 13 December 1981, 1, 28–30.

Kauffman, Stanley. "Some of Our Best Writers." *New York Times Book Review*, 30 May 1965, 1, 16–17.

Kazin, Alfred. *Contemporaries*. Boston: Little, Brown, 1962.

―――. "My Friend Saul Bellow." *Atlantic Monthly* 215 (January 1965): 51–54.

―――. "The Jew As Modern Writer." *Commentary* 41 (April 1966): 37–41.

―――. "The Earthly City of the Jews." In *The Bright Book of Life:*

American Novelists and Storytellers from Hemingway to Mailer, 125–63. Boston: Little, Brown, 1973.

Kenner, Hugh. "From Lower Bellowvia." *Harper's*, February 1982, 64–66.

Klein, Marcus. "Saul Bellow: A Discipline of Nobility." In *After Alienation: American Novels in Mid-Century*, 33–70. Cleveland: Meridian, 1965.

Knipp, Thomas R. "The Cost of Henderson's Quest." *Ball State University Forum* 10 (Spring 1969): 37–39.

Kostelanetz, Richard, ed. *On Contemporary Literature*. New York: Avon, 1964.

———. "Militant Minorities." *Hudson Review* 18 (Autumn 1965): 472–80.

Kulshrestha, Chirantan. *Saul Bellow: The Problem of Affirmation*. New Delhi, India: Arnold-Heineman, 1978.

Lainoff, Seymour. "American Jewish Fiction before the First World War." *Chicago Jewish Forum* 24 (Spring 1966): 207–17.

Landis, Joseph C. "Reflections on American Jewish Writers." *Jewish Book Annual* 21 (1967): 140–47.

Leach, Elsie. "From Ritual to Romance Again: *Henderson the Rain King*." *Western Humanities Review* 14 (Spring 1960): 223–24.

Levenson, J. C. "Bellow's Dangling Men." *Critique* 3 (Summer 1960): 3–14.

Liptzin, Solomon. *The Jew in American Literature*, 194–95. New York: Bloch, 1966.

Mailer, Norman. "Norman Mailer vs. Styron, Jones, Baldwin, Bellow, Heller, Updike, Burroughs, Salinger, Roth." *Esquire* 60 (July 1963): 64–69.

Majdiak, Daniel. "The Romantic Self and *Henderson the Rain King*." *Bucknell Review* 19 (Fall 1971): 125–47.

Malin, Irving. *Jews and Americans*. Carbondale: Southern Illinois University Press, 1965.

———. *Saul Bellow and the Critics*. New York: New York University Press, 1967.

———. *Saul Bellow's Fiction*. Carbondale: Southern Illinois University Press, 1969.

McSweeney, Henry. "Saul Bellow and the Life to Come." *Critical Quarterly* 18 (Spring 1976): 67–72.

Merkowitz, David Robert. *Bellow's Early Phase: Self and Society in "Dangling Man," "The Victim," and "The Adventures of Augie March."* Michigan, 1971, Marvin Felheim. DA XXXII-6439A.

Modern Fiction Studies (Special Bellow Issue) 25 (Spring 1979).

Moore, Harry T., ed. *Contemporary American Novelists*, 80–94. Carbondale: Southern Illinois University Press, 1964.

Morrow, Patrick. "Threat and Accommodation: The Novels of Saul Bellow." *Midwest Quarterly* 8 (Summer 1967): 389–411.

Moss, Judith P. "The Body as Symbol in Saul Bellow's *Henderson the Rain King.*" *Literature and Psychology* 20 (1970): 51–61.

Murdrick, Marvin. "Who Killed Herzog? or, Three American Novelists." *University of Denver Quarterly* 1 (Spring 1966): 61–97.

Nelson, Gerald B. *Ten Versions of America*. New York: Knopf, 1972.

Opdahl, Keith Michael. *The Novels of Saul Bellow: An Introduction*. University Park: Pennsylvania State University Press, 1967.

Overbeck, Pat T. "The Women in Augie March." *Texas Studies in Literature and Language* 10 (Fall 1968): 471–84.

Pearce, Richard. *Stages of the Clown: Perspectives on Modern Fiction from Dostoevsky to Beckett*. Carbondale: Southern Illinois University Press, 1970.

Pinsker, Sanford. "The Schlemiel in Yiddish and American Literature." *Chicago Jewish Forum* 25 (Spring 1967): 191–95.

———. "The Psychological Schlemiels of Saul Bellow." In *The Schlemiel as Metaphor: Studies in the Yiddish and American Jewish Novel*, 125–57. Carbondale: Southern Illinois University Press, 1971.

Podhoretz, Norman. "The New Nihilism in the American Novel." *Partisan Review* 25 (Fall 1958): 576–90.

———. "The Adventures of Saul Bellow." In *Doings and Undoings: The Fifties and After in American Writing*, 205–27. New York: Noonday Press, 1964.

Porter, H. Gilbert. "Herzog: A Transcendental Solution to an Existential Problem." *Forum* (Houston) 7 (Spring 1969): 32–36.

———. "*Henderson the Rain King*: An Orchestration of Soul Music." *New England Review* 6 (1972): 24–33.

———. *Whence Came the Power? The Artistry and Humanity of Saul Bellow*. New York: Columbia University Press, 1974.

Ribalow, Harold U. "What Happens to Jewish Writing?" *Congress Weekly* 16 (28 March 1949): 10–12.

———. "American Jewish Writers and Their Judaism." *Judaism* 3 (Fall 1954): 418–26.

———. "The Jewish Side of American Life." *Ramparts* 2 (Autumn 1963): 24–31.

———. "What's This Jewish Book Craze All About?" *National Jewish Monthly* 81 (November 1966): 50, 52.

Rodrigues, Eusebio L. "Bellow's Africa." *American Literature* 43 (May 1971): 242–56.

Rosenthal, T. G. "The Jewish Writer in America." *The Listener* 67 (12 April 1962): 635.

Roth, Philip. "The New Jewish Stereotypes." *American Judaism* 11 (Winter 1961): 10–11, 49–51.

———. "Writing American Fiction." *Commentary* 31 (March 1961): 223–33.

Rovit, Earl. *Saul Bellow*. Minneapolis: University of Minnesota Press, 1967.

Rubin, Louis D., Jr. "Southerners and Jews." *Southern Review* 2 (July 1966): 697–713.

Rupp, Richard H. "Saul Bellow: Belonging to the World in General." In *Celebration in Postwar American Fiction, 1945–1967*, 189–208. Coral Gables, Fla.: University of Miami Press, 1970.

Salmagundi (Special Bellow Issue) 30 (Summer 1975).

Salter, D. P. M. "Optimism and Reaction in Saul Bellow's Recent Work." *Critical Quarterly* 14 (Spring 1972): 57–66.

Sanderson, S. F. *Ernest Hemingway*. New York: Grove Press, 1961.

Sanes, Irving A., and Harvey Swados. "Certain Jewish Writers: Notes on Their Stereotype." *Menorah Journal* 37 (Spring 1949): 186–204.

Scheer-Schazler, Brigitte. *Saul Bellow*. Modern Literature Monographs. New York: Frederick Ungar, 1972.

Schueler, Mary D. "The Figure of Madeleine in *Herzog*." *Notes on Contemporary Literature* 1 (May 1971): 5–7.

Schulman, Elias. "Notes on Anglo-Jewish Writers." *Chicago Jewish Forum* 24 (Summer 1966): 276–80.

Schulman, Robert. "The Style of Bellow's Comedy." *PMLA* 83 (March 1966): 109–17.

Schultz, Max F. *Radical Sophistication: Studies in Contemporary Jewish-American Novelists*. Athens: Ohio University Press, 1969.

Scott, Nathan A., Jr. "Sola Gratia: The Principle of Bellow's Fiction." In *Adversity and Grace: Studies in Recent American Literature*, edited by Nathan A. Scott, Jr., 27–57. Chicago: University of Chicago Press, 1968.

Sherman, Bernard A. "The Jewish-American Initiation Novel." *Chicago Jewish Forum* 24 (Fall 1965): 10–14.

———. *The Invention of the Jew: Jewish-American Education Novels, 1916–1964*. New York: Thomas Yoseloff, 1969.

Solotaroff, Theodore. *The Red Hot Vacuum*. New York: Atheneum, 1970.

Stevenson, David L. "The Activists." *Daedalus* 92 (Spring 1963): 238–49.

Sutton, Henry. "Notes toward the Destitution of Culture." *Kenyon Review* 30 (1968): 108–15.

Tanner, Tony. *Saul Bellow*. Edinburgh: Oliver and Boyd, 1965.

———. "A Mode of Motion." In *City of Words: American Fiction 1950–1970*, 64–84. New York: Harper and Row, 1971.

Thompson, John. "A Vocal Group: The Jewish Part in American Letters." *Times Literary Supplement*, 6 November 1959, xxxv–xxxvi.

———. "The Fiction Machine." *Commentary* 46 (October 1968): 67–71.

Trachtenberg, Stanley. "Saul Bellow's *Luftmenschen*: The Compromise with Reality." *Critique* 9, no. 3 (1967): 37–61.

Trowbridge, Clinton W. "Water Imagery in *Seize the Day*." *Critique* 9, no. 3 (1968): 62–73.

Updike, John. "Draping Radiance with a Worn Veil." *New Yorker*, September 1975, 122–30.

Waldmeir, Joseph J. "Only an Occasional Rutabaga: American Fiction since 1945." *Modern Fiction Studies* 15 (Winter 1969–1970): 467–81.

Weber, Ronald. "Bellow's Thinkers." *Western Humanities Review* 22 (Autumn 1968): 305–13.

———. "Jewish Writing in America: Jewish or American?" *Ball State University Forum* 10 (Spring 1969): 40–49.

Weinberg, Helen. "Kafka and Bellow: Comparisons and Further Definitions"; "The Heroes of Saul Bellow's Novels." In *The New Novel in America: The Kafkan Mode in Contemporary Fiction*, 29–54, 55–107. Ithaca, N.Y.: Cornell University Press, 1970.

Wisse, Ruth. *The Schlemiel as Modern Hero*. Chicago: University of Chicago Press, 1971.

Index

"crisis history" (*Herzog*), 66,
96; contract (*Mr. Sammler's
Planet*), 69; "lessons of the
Real," 70, 74; "reality
instructor" (Corde), 120; con
men vs. tricksters, 135 (n. 5)

"A Silver Dish," 115
Stevens, Wallace, 6

Thoreau, Henry David, 29, 55,
83, 127
To Jerusalem and Back, 114
Transcendentalism: unique
artistic consciousness, 4, 9;
"eye," 6, 10; imagination,

122; romantic tradition, 126,
128
Tu As Raison Aussi, 40
Twain, Mark (Samuel Clemens),
38, 58
"Two Morning Monologues,"
13–14

Weinberg, Helen, 136 (n. 1)
Whitman, Walt, 7, 55; artist as
mystical namer, 4; *Leaves of
Grass*, 30; individual quests,
37
Wordsworth, William, 127,
137 (n. 1)

Young, Philip, 82, 87